Walter Rye

Pedes Finium

Fines, Relating to the County of Norfolk

Walter Rye

Pedes Finium

Fines, Relating to the County of Norfolk

ISBN/EAN: 9783743410497

Manufactured in Europe, USA, Canada, Australia, Japa

Cover: Foto ©ninafisch / pixelio.de

Manufactured and distributed by brebook publishing software (www.brebook.com)

Walter Rye

Pedes Finium

PEDES FINIUM:

OR

FINES,

Relating to the County of Norfolk,

LEVIED IN THE KING'S COURT
FROM THE THIRD YEAR OF RICHARD I. TO THE END OF
THE REIGN OF JOHN.

EDITED BY

WALTER RYE.

Norwich:

PRINTED BY A. H. GOOSE & CO.

(LATE MILLER AND LEAVINS),

1881.

Pedes Finium.

INTRODUCTION.

TOPOGRAPHERS have, I think, unaccountably neglected the mass of information which the *Feet of Fines* afford. The labour necessary to carefully go through the unindexed files is no doubt immense, but the results are so valuable that an account of a manor or locality is incomplete indeed without such labour being undertaken. As far as regards Norfolk, Le Neve no doubt supplied Blomefield with notes of most of the more important fines, so our county history is probably more perfect in this respect than any other; but there are many instances in which important topographical and genealogical facts have been passed over.[1] Moreover, at the time Le Neve was working so industriously, very slight interest was taken in families which were not or had not been in a knightly or gentle position, and no notes were taken by him of the names of the small freeholders, many of whose descendants are now of importance in the county. Nor did the *rariorum* readings of the names of localities, of the utmost value in tracing their

---

[1] For example, No. 1 fixes the date of the undated charter relating to the same transaction quoted at p. 308 of vol. x. of Blomefield; No. 9 enables us to correct Blomefield, who created a new abbot of St. Bennet's, by referring to "John" instead of Ralph; No. 36 mentions Hervey son of Hugh Le Strange, whose existence is not noticed by Blomefield or by the editor of the *Visitation;* No. 48 gives the parentage of Wm. de Redham, and so on.

derivation,[2] nor the immense wealth of field names, interest him in any way; indeed we may roughly say that if a fine did not chronicle the descent of a manor or advowson, or give some pedigree information about some armigerous family, it was passed by unnoted.

Nearly twenty years ago our Society began to print the Norfolk fines at length, with a translation and notes; but only a dozen fines were issued,[3] ably edited by the Rev. G. H. Dashwood. Owing, I believe, to the gentleman who supplied the copies of such twelve fines failing to send any more, their publication was dropped, and it was perhaps as well that it was so, for, published in this form, it would have taken about forty volumes the size of our Transactions to have completed them. I was subsequently asked to begin again in a tabular form, which, by omitting the formal parts of the document, has the advantage of giving five times as much information in the same space. For reasons into which I need not go now, though I may say that the delay has not been with me, the issue of these fines has been slow; but I am at last enabled to place in my readers' hands *précis* of the eight hundred and one fines relating to our county which were levied in the reigns of Richard I. and John, with indexes of the names and places which occur in them.

I believe this is the first time that the fines of any county have been seriously taken in hand, and I venture to hope that the results may induce others to work the fines of other counties.

---

[2] The science of tracing etymologies was in its infancy. Blomefield, or rather his continuator Parkin, had "water" on the brain: nearly every place-name according to him came from "water."

[3] These transcripts contained many inaccuracies, *e.g.*, in No. 3 de Nereford is printed de Hereford; in the consideration 20ˢ is misprinted 10ˢ; in No. 8 30ᵃ is printed 20ᵃ; in No. 11 Scule is printed Seale: and the place-names are spelt wrongly.

One discovery arising from the analysis is, I think, of very considerable importance, and that is that the fines for Norfolk vastly outnumber those of any other county. Indeed, for the reign of Richard I. Norfolk has 293, while Bedfordshire, Berkshire, Buckinghamshire, Cambridgeshire, Cumberland, Cornwall, Derbyshire, Devonshire, and Dorsetshire *together* only have 231.—Cooper *on Public Records*, ii. p. 431. Coupling this with the facts that in the Norfolk fines there is a much greater proportion relating to small holdings of five acres[4] and under than in any other county (a fact which points to numerous small freeholders),[5] and that in the early Norfolk fines now before us we come across an unusually large proportion of Scandinavian names, we are drawn to the conclusion that we have here strong evidence that the Norman kings were wise enough to leave their near kinsmen the Danes undisturbed in their holdings to a very much greater extent than has hitherto been suspected.

The point is so historically interesting that I hope I may be excused if I devote some considerable space to it. Perhaps as good a way to show the marked difference in race between the inhabitants of our county and those of some of the shires will be to print the following analysis of the Christian or fore-names occurring in the fines for Richard I. and John for Bedfordshire, Berkshire, and Buckinghamshire, which I have extracted, not without considerable trouble, from vol. i. of the printed fines published by the late Joseph Hunter for the Record Commission in 1835.

BEDFORDSHIRE (91.)

Abel	Alditha	Alienor	Aumaric
Adam	Alexander	Alviva	Avicia
Agnes	Alice	Amabel	Bartholomew
Albreda	Alicia	Arnold	Beatrix

[4] I have grave doubts whether an "acre" then was not much larger than the present acre. By the way, a "roda" was a *rood*, pp. 17, 20.

[5] Mr. Greenstreet reminds me that the enormous number of Norfolk entries on the *De Banco Rolls* bears out this.

Berenger	Gerinus	Lecia	Ralph
Bertram	Gilbert	Letecia	Reginald
Cecilia	Gregory	Maria	Richard
Claricia	Gunilda	Margeria	Robert
Cristiana	Heimeric	Matilda	Roesia
David	Henry	Mauger	Rohesia
Edelina	Herman	Michael	Roger
Editha	Hilary	Milo	Sarra
Egelina	Hubert	Natalia	Simon
Elena	Hugh	Nicholas	Stannive
Elias	Humphrey	Nigel	Stephen
Emma	Jocelin	Olimpiada	Thomas
Estrilda	Johanna	Osbert	Walter
Eustace	John	Pagan	Warin
Eva	Jordan	Patric	Wido
Felicia	Katherine	Peter	William
Geoffrey	Lairna	Petronilla	Wischard
Gerard	Laurence	Prudencia	

BERKSHIRE (90.)

Adam	Edward	Hawisia	Nigel
Agnes	Eleanor	Henry	Osbert
Aillina	Elias	Herbert	Petronilla
Akina	Emma	Hodierna	Philip
Alan	Ernald	Hugelina	Ralph
Alexander	Ernewi	Hugh	Richard
Alice	Eudo	Ilbert	Roesia
Alina	Eustace	Isabel	Robert
Almaric	Eva	Ivo	Roger
Alveva	Felicia	Johanna	Sarra
Amicia	Fulco	John	Sarvalus
Anastasia	Geoffrey	Jordan	Serlo
Andrew	Geramus	Juetta	Sibilla
Arnold	Gerard	Lambert	Silvester
Athone	Gerold	Leslina	Simon
Baldwin	Giles	Letitia	Stigand
Berenger	Gilbert	Mabilia	Thomas
Bernard	Ginda	Martin	Tiulphus
Cecilia	Golda	Matilda	Turebert
Costancia	Guinda	Matthew	Walter
Cristiana	Gunnora	Margaret	Warin
Editha	Hamelin	Nicholas	William
Edmund			

BUCKINGHAMSHIRE (105.)

Adam	Amabilia	Berner	Emma
Agnes	Amfria	Cecilia	Euticia
Ailrich	Amicia	Claricia	Fulco
Ala	Andrew	Clement	Geoffrey
Alan	Asketin	Constancia	Gerard
Alard	Aremaric	Cristiana	Giles
Alditha	Baldwin	David	Gilbert
Alexander	Basile	Edward	Gocelin
Alina	Basilia	Eilevysa	Godfrey
Alice	Benedict	Elias	Godwin
Alured	Bernard	Elizabetha	Gregory

v.

Gunilda	Lecia	Oliva	Rohosia
Hamo	Lemane	Osbert	Rolland
Hamund	Lubias	Pagan	Salumon
Hawisia	Mabilia	Peter	Sanson
Helewisia	Margena	Petronilla	Simon
Henry	Martin	Philip	Stephen
Herbert	Matilda	Quintin	Susana
Hugh	Matthew	Ralph	Thomas
Isabella	Maurice	Reginald	Trianus
James	Michael	Richard	Vielus
Jeva	Milo	Richent	Vitalis
Johanna	Muriell	Richer	Walter
John	Nicholas	Robert	Warin
Jordan	Nigel	Roesia	Wido
Juliana	Ocin [qy.Owen]	Roger	William
Lawrence			

With these lists of names, nearly all of which are familiar to the antiquary, I will now ask my readers to compare the extraordinary list[6] of Christian or fore-names from the Norfolk fines which is here subjoined, premising that very many of them are of sufficient rarity to have escaped the notice of Miss C. M. Yonge in her valuable work on *The History of Christian Names*.

NORFOLK (322 Names.)

Abric, 42
Acelina, 10
Achard, 8, 93
Achilchard, [used as surname] 114
Adeldreda, 98
Adelstan, 32
Ædwin, 26
Aildive, 26
Aildrick, 58
Ailed, 52
Ailleth, 32
Ailmer, 50
Ailric, 34
Ailrich, 45
Ailward, 10, 28
Ainalda, 10
Aki, 17
Aleluri (?), 22
Aleysia, 126
Alfwin, 104
Algar, 58
Aluric, 22
Alveva, 30 bis.
Amindus, 46

Angod, 62
Armeniard, 106
Arnild, 94
Asalac, 28
Aselac, 50
Asketel, 30, 34
Astin, 74
Astyn, 130
Athelward, 78
Atketel, 38
Aubertus, 64
Aured, 42
Avand, 40
Avant (?), 30
Ave, 50
Baldehiva, 32
Basilica, 78
Bela, 26, 72
Blakeman, 84
Blakewin, 20
Bonde, 12 (?)
Boselinus, 84
Botilda, 8, 40, 58
Braies, 89
Brialed, 12

Bricce, 107
Bricthuā, 94
Brictmar, 45
Britrich, 24
Brogo, 96
Brunā, 12
Bruniswein, 32
Brunsewein, 22 bis
Bund, 64
Bunde, 104
Burdi, 108
Closwein, 120
Costinus, 70
Costar, 84
Costion, 80
Cruis, 40
Currichīt, 130
Cuti (?), 26
Dameta, 114
Damia (?), 99
Dering, 10
Dove, 48
Durand, 20, 122
Durant, 90
Ede, 58

[6] To save space I have omitted all common and well-known names, such as William, John, &c.

Edift, 122
Ediva, 110
Edric, 34, 123
Edrith, 104
Elebald, 8
Eleured, 84
Elfleda, 40, 42, 74
Elflet, 132
Elfnoth, 74
Elfreda, 34
Elinne, 10
Elviva (? Elvina), 74, 92
Elwin, 34, 115
Emelina, 48
Emeloc, 72
Engeleda, 52
Engelieth, 32
Erneburga, 136
Esole, 74
Estilda, 108
Espeland, 56
Estmund, 26
Estrilda, 110
Eund (?), 24
Eva, 28
Evis, 8
Fraer, 46
Frari, 28
Fredon, 94
Fulcher, 30
Fulcho, 7
Fulered, 40
Geleran(i), 116
Gena, 114
Gerberg, 66
Gerbode, 131
Goda, 36, 84
Godard, 30
Godein, 12
Goding, 82, 93, 129
Godiva, 36, 40, 54, 74
Godric, 74
Godwin, 66, 84
Goldruñ (female), 10
Gomel, 54
Gosse, 34
Goucy, 112
Goutr', 24
Guña, 40
Gunilda, 40
Gutfrith, 54
Guynilda, 36
Haco, 108
Haie, 80
Hakun, 24
Haldan, 128
Haldein, 10
Hamond, 28
Hane, 52
Hardewin, 26, 130

Hardwin, 10, 16
Harlewin, 34
Harvey, 24
Hawis (male), 26
Heloin, 34
Helye, 10
Helvisa, 12
Hereward, 54
Herlewin, 10
Herman, 34
Hervald (? Hernald), 42
Hervey, 26
Hodierna, 22, 40
Honfr', 12
Houward, 34
Howard, 10, 96
Huetred, 26
Huelin, 74
Hulf, 88
Ibert, 126
Iling, 110
Imbria, 12
Inca, 64
Incta, 122
Inetta, 82
Ingeleth, 94
Isolda, 22, 139
Jurnet, 67
Ketell, 26, 54
Langlina, 40
Lecelina, 8, 22
Lecenta, 132
Lefcini, 50
Lefli, 30, 40, 50, 116
Lefwin, 92, 94, 104
Leinan, 67
Leofwin, 108
Leowin, 44
Lesquen, 124
Leuric, 10
Leuwine, 34
Leva, 50
Levare, 40
Leve, 24, 38
Levesun, 122
Leveve, 26
Levive, 8, 48
Levinie, 40
Leurie, 10
Lewand, 58
Livena, 112
Lucent, 17
Mabel, 112
Macelin, 124
Marcellina, 124
Mazelina, 136
Mazeline, 110
Morand', 94
Morant, 40
Odbert, 40

Ode, 106
Offing, 10
Oki, 40
Ordwi (?), 164
Orrich, 122
Osegod, 30
Osegot, 43
Osketel, 36
Otewie, 102
Other, 34
Ourverd, 32
Parmel, 139
Piwith, 79
Reiner, 24
Ribald, 44
Richer, 72
Richilda, 56
Riguare, 54
Rigware, 40
Rikolf, 52
Rixxe, 84
Rod', 57
Runilda, 30
Safred, 70, 88
Saffrei, 82
Safrei, 54
Salerna, 84
Seipard, 79
Seriotbi (?) 74
Seul, 127
Seule, 9, 10, 34
Sedegos, 42
Sefugel, 116
Sefugell, 38
Segelin, 36
Segviun or Seguinn, 101
Selvest'r, 88
Semann, 86
Sigar, 34
Sigenild, 12
Siredd, 108
Sirache, 78
Siric, 36
Siward, 40
Stanard, 81
Stangrun, 22, 32
Steingrun, 90
Stanild, 54
Stannard, 88
Staumer, 38
Sturmi, 12
Sugband (?), 74
Sumered, 86
Suneman, 88
Swan, 82
Swani, 17
Swarin, 22
Swartagar, 92
Swein, 58
Swenild, 67

Swetive, 118
Swetemā, 124
Swetman, 63, 54
Thede, 86
Thedric, 54
Thieda, 44, 68
Thoke, 54, 74
Tholy, 72
Thorad, 34
Thurbert, 40
Thure, 54
Thurgand (female), 88
Thurketell, 22
Thurkil, 10
Thurold, 26
Thurstan, 22, 30, 40
Toch', 54
Toke, 38, 72
Token, 38
Torald, 108
Torold, 72
Torrond, 16
Tovi, 96
Turber, 118
Turgis, 60
Turild, 30
Turketel, 30
Turkil, 102
Turstan, 40
Turstein, 42
Turvis, 57
Ulf, 24, 26, 30, 86
Ulfketell, 98
Ulfus, 8
Vacilla, 131
Villiam, 78
Vivien, 44
Wakelin, 42
Waren, 24
Warin, 128
Waringer, 103
Warner, 98
Werbald, 12
Wic, 34
Wictieve, 30
Wider, 17
Wigot, 10
Wimar, 58
Winnarca, 128
Wimer, 32
Wimunde, 52
Windlevi (?), 116
Wither, 73
W(u lfach, 68
Wulfyat, 82
Wulmar, 50
Wulnard, 52
Wulnad, 13
Wulnod, 24
W(u)luric, 30
Wulvave, 54
W(u)lveve, 26
W(u)lviva, 40
W(u lvive, 8, 46
Wulvivia, 40
Wymer, 26
Ysmaina, 62
Yward, 129

I need hardly point out that a very large proportion indeed of these names are Scandinavian, and reference to the Index at the end of this publication will also show very many surnames of Scandinavian origin, *e.g.*, Anketel, Bacun, Atketel, Ketel, Thurkil, and Thurold.

The Norman and other continental names which occur are not as numerous as would be expected by those who fancy that the Norman Conquest literally flooded all England with Normans and Frenchmen. Of course many of the A filius B entries were meant for A "Fitz" B, so it is difficult to ascertain exactly what numerical proportion of the landowners were Norman; but I do not think that more than 110 Norman or French names[7] occur in the 801 fines.

But, however the people came by their names, it is very interesting to find in a list of surnames occurring more than six hundred years ago such every-day Norfolk names as

---

[7] It is of course hard to say in some cases whether the names were those of Normans who still bore Danish names, or of Danes who had come over direct, *e.g.*, Tholy Waco, Ulf Lovel, Warin, &c.

Bacon, Bayfield, Barrett, Burrell, Caley, Cobb, Colman, Cooper, Hammond, Durrand, Goss, Gurney, Lomb, Reyner, Rye, Rix, Swan, Swatman, Thirkettle, Tuck, Ulf, and Walpole.

The rarity of nicknames or by-names is remarkable. All I have come across are about twenty, viz., Godsaule,[8] le Cat, Wudecok, Cobbe, Swan, Cuckuc, Heron, Crowe, le Neuman, Kinesman, Wisman, Freman, Yvvelhume, le Blund, le Brun, le Gris, Pauper, le Gay, le Wile, le Curteis, and le Gros.

Nor are the trade or occupation names as numerous as might have been expected, viz., Mercator and le Marchand, Faber, Bisop and Biscop, Clericus, Sacerdos, Diachonus, le Moinne, Cocus, Feutrarius, Falconar, Forester, Bedell, Carpentarius and Carpenter, Parmentarius, Camerarius, Hostiarius, Janitor, Pincerna, Molendarius, le Flittere, le Norreis, le Spicer, le Eschermisur, le Fevere, le Veautre, &c.

As, roughly speaking, about one thousand and fifty varieties of names occur among the parties, attorneys, and tenants, in the fines printed hereafter, it is rather strange that not quite 3 per cent. of them should be nicknames or trade names. Of the remainder, about two hundred and forty were of the type "A the son of B," about fourteen were single names, such as "Ivo," and the rest for the most part were of the form "John of Snoring,"[9] "Hugh of Skerdeston."

So far I have dealt with the people and their names—we now come to the localities mentioned in the fines. Not the least reward of the dry labour of indexing was the discovery of over fifty localities which cannot now be traced in the county, and which escaped even the research of

---

[8] Which after all may only be a corruption of Godselhage.

[9] Variations are rare, but two may be noted, "William Boidi son of Robert" (p. 118), and Alan de Englefield, otherwise filius Muriell (p. 132).

Mr. Munford.[1] It may be convenient to give a separate list of them here, with some remarks opposite each.

Alingeton, 15. Possibly Illington: there are two Allingtons in Lincolnshire.
Aracton, 129.
Beneytleia, 117. Query Bentley in Suffolk.
Billingesbi, 113. There is a Billingborough in Lincolnshire: cf. Billingford (bis) and Billockby.
Blakeworde, 11. Query Blackworth in Northumberland.
Bodokesham, 125 bis.
Chedestane, 91. Query Kerdeston: cf. Chedgrave: query Chediston in Suffolk.
Cherwelleston, 87.
Chilveston, 83.
Clippesthorp, 103: cf. Clippesby.
Cotes, 83.
Diewude, 75: cf. Dickleborough.
Dinnenethoū, 129.
Dudwic, 55.
Dunstale, 55. Query Dunstable in Bedford.
Egleston, 9. There is "Eagle" in Lincoln.
Erwelestun, 95.
Ess, 131.
Estmora, 133.
Finchele, 71: cf. Fincham.
Glosebreg, 9: cf. Glosthorpe.
Grenesvill, 11. There is a Greenfield in Lincoln.
Grovele (query), 85.
Hatchetot, 133: cf. Hackford.
Haringeshang, 97: cf. Herringby.
Heveye, 129.
Hikeford, 35. Query Hackford: cf. Hickling.
Horstun, 497: cf. Horsley—ford—ham—stead.
Humersfield, 61. Homersfield in Suffolk, query.
Illegrave, 121. Query H. possibly Hilgay.
Inland, 87. Query near Gateley.
Karboisthorp, 37: cf. Garboldisham. There is a Garthorpe in Lincolnshire.
Kikelington, 29. Query H.
Kinesthorp, 59.
Knardeston, 83.
Kyneholm, 55: cf. Cowholm, Norwich Priory.
Langwade, 41. Possibly Lenwade.
Lowingeham, 59.
Nesse, 9.
Neuwater, 11.
Norcot, 85.
Northton, 9. Query Burnham Norton.
Rocton, 11: cf. Rockland.

[1] I have referred in each case to the original fine to be sure that it has not been misplaced from the bundle of another county.

Sailtwert, 127.
Socestone (query), 107
Stikingeland, 105.
Sudmere, 57
Tering or Toring, 9. Query Terrington.
Torpingemers, 117.
Tunethorp, 111: *cf.* Tunstall.
Wicherestorp, 83.
Wicclesford, 107. Query Wickford in Essex.

Of these, eleven are clearly Danish, viz., Billinges*by*, Clippes*thorp*, Dud*wic*, Ille*grave*, Karbois*thorp*, Kines*thorp*, Kyne*holm*, *Nesse*, *Torpinge*mers, Tune*thorp*, and Wicheres*torp*; and it is just possible they were names of villages which were dropped as the Danes left their neighbourhood. Nesse may have been off Foulness by Cromer, and be now lost in the sea like Shipden and Eccles. Of the others, three, viz., Bentley, Chediston, and Homersfield, are in Suffolk, and Dunstable is in Essex, and yet the fines in which they occur are clearly marked "Norf" in a cotemporary hand. So is another (p. 91), which obviously relates to Tilbury in Essex.

More interesting still are the very numerous field-names, of which no less than four hundred occur. As charters and deeds of this date are very rare, and when they do occur seldom do more than specify the name of the manor or advowson conveyed, I have thought it worth while to arrange these names under headings as well as I can, asking my reader to treat leniently my versions of hitherto unknown places, which will no doubt receive many corrections from abler hands.

The list affords a tempting field for conjecture, but, being no "scollard," I will leave this to others, and will only point out that we may recognize here many of our favourite field-names, such as Fouracres, Sevenacres, and Twelveacres; Homefield, Northfield, and Westfield. Many of the "gates" would seem to refer to the way to or direction of an adjacent village, *e.g.*, Brancastergate, Stanhoegate, and Wintertongate.

xi.

Some of the names are unmercifully long, *e.g.*, Blacunldehevedland, Burwennesneuheland, Kaimluesmerehevedland, Dudegraveuverwang, and Dunchersseswang. Can the latter have meant the dun horse's wang?

Acre.
  Benehalfacre, 95
  Fouracres, 19
  Helwinesacre, 41
  Hevedacre, 81
  Knapewellaera, 73
  Longehalfaker, 115, 117
  Rodulvesaker, 39
  Schortehalfacre, 95
  Schirevesacre, 125
  Sevenacre, 123
  Sevenacris, 29
  Sunndesacre, 139
  Twelfacres, 99
  Wildeker, 71

Beach, or Bech.
  Bech, 79
  Ratlesbech, 63
  Redhebech, 115
  Waxsebeche, 131

Brakes.
  West Brakes, 77

Bridge.
  Prestebrige, 61

Broom.
  Brom, 37
  Brome, 75
  Michelbrom, 125

Bury.
  Beveresbure, 39
  Lingmiddelberg, 99
  Stanberh, 91

Bush.
  Lāhābush, 59 (? Langham bush)

Busks.[2]
  Aslakebusk, 103
  Two buskes, 81

By.
  Billingesbi, 113

Cot.
  Lambecot, 39

Croft.
  Adverescroft, 121
  Ailevescroft, 125
  Alevescroft, 125
  Alvodescroft, 37
  Barlicroft, 17
  Būbelescroft, 37
  Beterhuscroft, 137
  Bunegerescroft, 65
  Bunescroft, 45
  Colecroft, 59
  Colescroft, 72
  Craucroft, 113
  Croft, 73
  Crophto, 95
  Estecroft, 21
  Ethstanescroft, 113
  Fruntescroft, 129
  Gailecroft, 55
  Geggiscroft, 15
  Gittiscroft, 15
  Godwinescroft, 135
  Grasecroft, 87
  Hachenescroft, 101
  Harescroft, 39
  Hestecroft, 101 (? East Croft)
  Hethincroft, 17
  Hobbescroft, 41
  Hudiscroft, 25
  Katecroft, 77
  Kilnecroft, 45
  Kingescroft, 137
  Lillardescroft, 37
  Linecroft, 25
  Millicroft, 45
  Piggescroft, 103
  Pottescroft, 19
  Pratescroft, 133
  Ranescroft, 125
  Ridecroft, 43
  Riecroft, 43
  Silescroft, 51

Tuicroft (?), 37
Wudecroft, 117

Cross.
  Broccross, 95

Crundel.
  Gatlecrundel, 39
  Slokrundel, 77

Dale.
  Bradale, 59
  Cademanesdale, 35
  Dimigedal, 61
  Hartesdal, 9
  Hungerdale, 57
  Scodale (?), 113

Dele.
  Bolohogedel, 51
  Crokelundele, 39
  Kirkedele, 47
  Manhondele, 77
  Suinesdele, 25
  Trendele, 105
  Weistdele, 25

Delf.[3]
  Hildelf, 101

Dich, or Dike.
  Burgdich, 95
  Dich, 75
  Lowedich, 81
  Treisdikes, 103
  Widehagedig, 35

Den.
  Yotenden, 95

Don.
  Hameldon, 9
  Langedon, 23

End.
  Hildikesende, 101
  Holegates end, 67

Fallgate.
  Pakkeresfaillate, 127

---

[2] Buske or Busshe, *Prompt. Parv.*, 56

[3] Delph, a drain which empties itself into a larger drain—a dyke which has been delved —Brogden's *Provincial Words of Lincolnshire*.

Fen.
  Allewellefen, 83
  Mickelfen, 85

Field.
  Humesfeld, 61 (? the Home Field)
  Northfeld, 77, 119
  Westfeld, 119

Fleet.[4]
  Alfladeflet, 91
  Meresflet, 101

Ford.
  Heaghenhildford, 71
  Ilneford, 51
  Sentford, 80

Furlong.
  Brantesfurlang, 61
  Gavelefurlinges, 23
  Langefurlang, 117
  Michelemadfurlong, 129
  Northfurlang, 57
  Suthmorfurlang, 61

Gate.
  Abunesgate, 95
  Akergate, 77
  Bergate, 97
  Bradegate, 55
  Brancestregate, 69
  Brechegate, 95
  Chirchegat, 95
  Cranewissegat, 89
  Creiegate, 25
  Estgate, 95
  Feltwellegat, 89
  Grenegate, 77
  Harthornesgate, 19
  Herpelegate, 51
  Hescogate, 107
  Holandegat, 55
  Holegate, 103
  Kirkegate way, 93
  Langhāgate, 59
  Litleholgat, 105
  Marlingate, 95
  Nowetongate, 39
  Northgate, 139
  Nungate, 97
  Rigeweigate, 77
  Sepegate, 119
  Stanhoegate, 87

Sumringate, 121
Suthwadhegate, 97
Uveregate, 127
Wellegate, 55
Westegate, 115
Westgate, 117, 121
Wetingate, 91
Wintertunegate, 49
Witegate, 31
Wodegate, 59

Grave.[5]
  Aiegrave, 39
  Bertigrave, 101
  Dudegrave, 117
  Lambigrave, 57
  Wlngrave, 81

Hage or Hoge.
  Bruneshage, 43
  Frunteshage (wood), 129
  Greneg, 113
  Haringeshag, 97
  Hoddehoge, 49
  Langetheihage, 137
  Ridehage, 133
  Stanahage, 125
  Wadhoge, 39

Hay.[6]
  Hermitesheie, 63
  Exhaiz, 81
  Rugunerhae, 101

Hall.
  Hiringeshal, 25
  Rutlingehal, 15
  Stanhal, 55

Head.
  Heued, 75
  Onecoteshed, 95

Hill.
  Alwineshill, 61
  Asgereshill, 107
  Atterhill, 77
  Galterhill, 127
  Hovekeshill, 97
  Holegatehill, 37
  Leirgravehill, 113
  Linghill, 95
  Norhhill, 45
  Quenhill, 19

Scridehill, 37
Snareshill, 99
Suthill, 107
'Upon the Hill,' 45

Hole, or Hales.
  Foxhales, 125
  Foxhole, 83
  Muckole, 133

Holm.
  Brakeholm, 141
  Brakenholm, 23
  Crosholm, 25
  Henundesholm, 99
  Holme, 19
  Nieweholm, 25

Ho, or How.
  Bahardeshowe, 55
  Blacheho, 59
  Calculneshowe, 87
  Erdehou, 125
  Galecho, 125
  Hedenesho, 137
  Langeroe, 85
  Milnehoe mersh, 97
  Mulehou, 37
  Packelowe, 59
  Sewardescroe, 137
  Stanhou, 139
  Wiccericheshoue, 35

Ing.
  Estldefridding, 77
  Liteling, 101
  Nordinge, 17
  Spolinges, 39
  Wadinges, 63

Lane.
  Netherlaine, 39

Ling.
  Spolinges, 39
  Spotlinges, 39

Lond, or Land.[7]
  Blacunldehevedland, 139
  Blakeland, 99
  Bradeland, 129
  Brendeland, 99
  Brodeland, 29
  Buclond, 37
  Burland, 133

---

[4] A salt water tidal creek.

[5] No doubt used in the sense of ditch or trench, Danish *grav*.

[6] "Still used in Norfolk for a hedge."—Halliwell's *Dictionary*.

[7] Also see "ad longam terram" and "ad curtam terram," at p. 45.

BurwennesNeuheland, 41
Buscland, 115
Crundeland, 53
Eldeland, 117
Estlangelond, 39
Evedlond, 77
Gilbert's land, 95
Gorland, 119
Haxland, 85
Inland, 87
Kaimluesmereheved-land, 105
Langedonohavetlond, 23
Langedon Brembelond, 23
Langeland, 87, 105
Lund, 57
Milneland, 21
Netherlond, 115
Neuloond, 75
Pacewineslund, 45
Radeland, 63
Redeland, 39
Rotilond, or Roulond, 101
Sandlond, 21
Sandland, 77
Sanland, 113
Schorteland, 95
Snakesland, 77
Sorteland, 9
Sortehardlond, 61
Sternelond, 21
Stornlond, 117
Swersland, 91
Taseburgland, 127
Wrogiland, 23

Meadow, Mede.
Witemedes, 17
Estmedewe, 49

Mers, or Mere.
Godinesmers, 115, 117
Torpinggemers, 117
Flaxmere, 133
Fresmere, 119
Hevedemere, 55
Ingemer, 133
Kirkemere, 113
Prestemere, 73, 131
Selimere, 95
Selomere, 95
Wadmar, 75
Wetingate merr, 91

Mill.
Bridge mill, 81
Erlesmilne, 71
Hundemilhe, 45
(? The Hundred mill)
Mersmelne, 135
Skerehunger mill, 139
Uvermilne, 29
William's mill, 85

Mor.
Estmor, 61
Estmore, 97
Kirbemor, 23
Notolnesmor, 119

Nab.
Wunstanesnab, 133

Pit.
Alderfanpittes, 123
Colput, 103
Greiputtes, 103
Grepittes, 119
Lampit, 127

Rod.
Herolfvesrode, 93
Witmererod, 53

Slade.[8]
Beeslade, 95
Merslades, 17

Spinney.
The Spinney, 83

Sty.
Berchenestie (?), 115
Beretrenestie (?), 117
Didelstie, 95
Grenestie, 95
Humstie, 95
Medelesties, 73
Sidesternesti, 25

Thorn.
Colebythorn, 89
Smalethornes, 55

Thorp.
Brunsthorp, 47
Poketorp, 107

Toft.
Bremestoft, 25
Edwinestofta, 95
Ethstanestoft, 113
Grisetoft, 27
Hafketelestofta, 95
Kinesmannestoft, 99
Offrichestoft, 69
Piggestoft, 125
Toftes, 43, 49
Udostoft, 33
Ulnestuft, 81
Ulvestoft, 89
Westtoft, 131

Town's end.
Westgate tonend, 57

Tun.
Muletun, 79

Well.
Kenting welle, or Kemingwelle, 89
Litlewell, 129
Scarbotewell, 63
Suthewelle, 95

Wong, or Wang.[9]
Blackswong, 123
Dudegraveuverwang, 117
Duneherssewang, 137
Ellernewong, 119
Munekeswong, 37
Netherwong, 117
Suineswong, 25
Uverswong, 115

Wood.
Fredeswude, 95
Hakeford wad, 115
Westwude, 105

Wro.
Killingewro, 49

---

[8] Variously explained; by Halliwell as a valley and a plain: the latter seems right.

[9] The Danish wang, a meadow.

Unidentified Places.

Alfwancsherne, 123	Greneg, 113	Sewardescroe, 137
Allesell, 125	Hech', 25	Siwatesfot, 123
Berch, 115	Hes, 49	Stanaue, 97, [? Stanhow]
Berchenestic (? Beretrevestic), 115, 117	Heued, 75	
	Hocee, 25	Stauberh, 91
Breche, le, 129	Iscris, 21	Sudbroc, 117
Brith, 25	La Drave, 63	Sirmecopt, 103
Cockesseg, 95	Leavines, 55	Ti'wate, 37
Drave, La, 63	Lochus, 123	Twisler, 75
Fortleg, 59	Lukedonhel, 69	Wadegrote, 125
Foxhalls, 125	Miclowcye, 125	Westmad, 125
Freduc, ad, 75	Ridehage, 133	Westris, 133
Gateschiles, 39	Rediz, 79	Wileghes, 105.
Gosegras, 133	Ringenuse, 53	Wilgeshik, 95

Occasionally we find in the fines entries interesting for many reasons. Thus Humphry de Herlham in 8 Ric. I. sold, for a hundred shillings, land to Ralph de Herlham (possibly his brother), for his equipment to Jerusalem, probably in the fifth Crusade then being instituted by Pope Innocent III.; and the objection naturally felt by large landowners to their sub-tenants giving land into mortmain, which did no service, is well instanced by Eva, daughter of Hawis de Morlai, granting lands to Ralph de Torcy and his assigns—" præterquam viris religiosis." Other instances of this exception will be found at pp. 35 and 69. Vineyards are mentioned at p. 137.

The nominal or unusual considerations are also interesting, *e.g.*, a pound of pepper (pp. 13, 67, 69, 85, 87, and 97); a pound of cummin (pp. 21, 49, 53, and 77); a pound of incense (p. 99); a pair of gloves (p. 139); a pair of white gloves (p. 13); a hawk (pp. 65, 87); a hawk of the first year (p. 15); a pair of gilt spurs worth 6*d.* (p. 21); four barbed arrows (p. 87); two horses (p. 25); a black horse of the third and another of the sixth year (p. 87); a horse worth 10 marks and the return of a deed (p. 119); a robe worth 2 marks (p. 117); a mantle and tunic (p. 33); two dresses and a gold ring (p. 51); two mallards (p. 27); two capons at Christmas (p. 139); a bullock (p. 105); 6,200 "sticks" of eels (p. 103); freedom from toll (p. 61); a gold ring and participation in the benefits of a monastery (p. 51); and similar participation without a ring (pp. 97, 135, and 139). An early instance of "liquidation by arrangement" will be found at p. 137, where a creditor releases a debtor who owes him 30 marks for a cash payment of 3 marks. The consideration is occasionally absent (p. 127), but its most usual forms are—

1. CASH, or cash and regrant of part of the land in fee, or cash and life annuity, or cash and rent (*i.e.*, purchase of a perpetual lease at a premium.)
2. EXCHANGE for other land, or exchange for other land and cash, or exchange for other land for which rent is to be paid (*i.e.*, exchange of freehold for leasehold.)
3. RENT, or rent and the grant of some other property, or a year's profits, or a release of arrears of rent.
4. An ANNUITY in perpetuity or for life.
5. The REGRANT for life at a rent or free of rent (*i.e.*, a loan for life.)
6. The REGRANT of part absolutely (*i.e.*, a partition.)
7. The REGRANT of part subject to a rent or service.

Instances of persons not parties to the fine taking benefits by it will be found at pp. 51, 55 (Nos. 237, 266); and the reader will find numerous cases in which the "calling to warrant" fiction occurs, thus showing how much earlier it was in existence than the invention of recoveries.

A few words on the Feet of Fines themselves may not be inappropriate.[1] They are written in a very small writing

---

[1] A very early Norfolk fine, not bound up with the series here indexed, is dated 35 Henry II. By it Wm. de Curzun grants a messuage in Norwich to Jornetus the Jew, in consideration of a cash payment of 5 marks and an annual payment of 5s. See *Hunter's Fines*, p. 23.

on pieces of parchment about as long as, but narrower than one's hand, indented or notched along the top, and are as a rule in good condition.

From the following exact transcript of one of them a better idea of their form and contractions may be gleaned than from any description, however ample.

H ✠ finał 9cord fēa In Cur̃ Dn̄i Reg̃ ap̄ Norwic̄ Anno Regni Ŗ Ric̄ vij° Die Sabb festo Sc̄e Marḡ Corā Witł de Glāvill ⁊ Osƀ fił Huic̄ ⁊ Sim̄ de Patesh Justic̄ Dn̄i Reg̃ ⁊ Alijs fidelib; Dn̄i Reg̃ ⁊c ibid p̄sentib; Int̃ Roƀ de Hickford pet̃ ⁊ Adā de Nereford ten̄ de . viij . acr̃ c̄ ptin̄ ī Spham . un̄ assa' de morte an̄cessoris su'mon̄ fuit Int̃ eos ī cur̃ p̄fata : Scił qd id Adā cōcessit eid Roƀ ⁊ hedib⁹ suis totā p̄dcām tr̃a cū ptin̄ tenend de se ⁊ hēdib; suis ! Reddendo In̄ an̄uatī sex denar̃ ad fest' Sc̄i Mich̃ . ⁊ ad xx . soł de Scutaḡ : vi d ⁊ ad plus ! plus . ⁊ ad min⁹ ! min⁹ p̄ ōi 9suetudine : ⁊ p h̄ᵃ cōcessone id Roƀ ded' dc̄o Ade tria Bizantia
Norf⁹

The above extended reads thus—

Hec est finalis concordia facta in curia Domini Regis apud Norwicum anno regni Regis Ricardi septimo, die Sabbati festo Sancte Margarete, Coram Willelmo de Glanvill et Osberto filio Hervici et Simone de Pateshill, Justiciariis Domini Regis, et aliis fidelibus Domini Regis &c. ibidem presentibus. Inter Robertum de Hickford petentem, et Adam de Nereford tenentem, de 8 acris cum pertinentiis in Sparham. Unde Assisa de morte antecessoris summonita fuit inter eos in curia prefata; scilicet quod idem Adam concessit eidem Roberto et heredibus suis totam predictam terram cum pertinentiis Tenendam de se et heredibus suis : Reddendo inde annuatim sex denarios ad festum Sancti Michaelis, et ad 20 solidos de xvii.

scutagio sex denarios, et ad plus plus et ad minus minus, pro omni consuetudine. Et pro hac concessione idem Robertus dedit dicto Ade tria bizantia.

Norfolchia.

And translated, thus—

This is the final agreement made in the Court of (our) Lord the King at Norwich on the Sabbath day, in the feast of St. Margaret, in the 7th year of King Richard, before William de Glanvill, Osbert Fitz Hervey, and Simon de Pateshill, Justices of (our) Lord the King, and other faithful (servants) of (our) Lord the King, &c., there present, between Robert de Hickford (the) demandant, and Adam de Nereford (the) tenant of eight acres with (their) appurtenances in Sparham, concerning which an assize of mort d'auncestor was summoned between them in the aforesaid court.

Namely, that the said Adam granted to the said Robert and his heirs all the aforesaid land with (its) appurtenances. To hold of him and his heirs, paying therefor yearly sixpence, and for every twenty shillings of scutage sixpence, and for more more and for less less, for all service.

And the said Robert for this grant gives to the said Adam three bezants.

Norfolk.

None of the Fines for Norfolk have been printed except in the experiment already mentioned.

The volumes published by the Record Commission in 1835—44 under the title of "Fines sive Pedes Finium," reach only to Beds, Bucks, and a few other counties whose initial letters are early in the alphabet.

Nor, from their commencement until the 1st Henry VIII.,

are there any public indices whatever to them.[2] Anterior to the last-named date the fines themselves[3] must be searched; unless reference is made to the Lansdowne MSS. 306, 307, and 308, which are apparently the original calendars, or entry books for the reigns of Edward III., Richard II., Henry IV., and Henry V., and which are easier to search.

From the 25th Henry VIII., however, the *Index to* (the Notes or duplicates of) *the Fines*, which gives short notices of the fines of each term arranged under the counties to which they belong, becomes available.

Up to the 32nd George II. these indices give the Christian names of the parties, and the name of the locality as well.

From the 1st George III., however, the entries run thus—

Bell | Townley | Millett

Millett being the attorney's name. These indices being, though not alphabetical, easy to search, are of course very valuable.

The Books of Entries of Fines, which extend from 1611, are arranged in a similar way to the last-named series, but give a little more information, viz., the entry mentioned above in them stands thus—

297. Henry Bell esq Plt & William Townley & Mary his wife & others Defts in Wrettone—Millett.

But the chief use of them is that the late volumes of this

---

[2] There certainly are a few (eleven) volumes, purporting to be indices to fines, which have been noted by private collectors, chiefly Le Neve, but these refer to so infinitesimally small a portion of the fines that they are perfectly useless. Some counties, it is true, have separate indices to some of their fines, but I only know of those I have myself compiled for Richard I., John, Henry III., Edward I., Henry VII., Henry VIII., Edward VI., and Mary. Most of these are to names only, and the last three are printed in Vol. II. of the *Norfolk Antiquarian Miscellany*.

[3] Which are bound up in thin bundles or parts of twenty-five.

series give references to the actual number borne by the Fines.

Lastly, the *King's Silver Books* (which exist from the reign of Henry VIII., but owing to damage done them by fire are inconsultable until that of George 1.) give yet more information about the property and parties, *e.g.*, the above referred to entry is thus extended.

20/. *Norfolk*   Henry Bell Esqre Plt Wm Townley &   13/4
8 St Hil   Robt Thorpe & Ann Mary his wife defts of 2 mess 1 barn 1 sta 2 cur 2 gar 1 or 20 La 20 mea 20 pas & com of pass for all mann of catt with the app^{ts} in Wretton & Stoke ffery Bfore Harvey Goodwin & Jno Houchen gents by com 29 Decr 38 K Geo 3

Other ways of getting references to fines there are, as by searching the *Extracts from Writs of Covenant* (Alienation Office), of which there are one hundred and thirty-five volumes, commencing 1576 (Index to same dating from 1661); and the *Concords of Fines* (Common Pleas), which begin Mich. 1, 2 Elizabeth; but as they are generally more troublesome to find, and give less satisfactory information when found, I think the three series above detailed will suffice for the amateur genealogist.

WALTER RYE.

Selhurst.

Note.—The party before whose name a star (*) is placed is in each case the grantor—or technically he who "quits claim."

ERRATA.

		for	read	
Page	13,	ij monialibʒ	et monialibʒ.	
	21	,, cinnamon	,, cummin.	
	31	,, Brentham?	,, Brettenham.	
	32	,, Brumswein	,, Bruinswein?	
	32	,, Stangim	,, Stangrin?	
	34	,, Helom	,, Heloin?	
	47	,, Wallingham	,, Walsingham.	
	57	,, Westgaletonēd	,, Westgattonēd.	
	59	,, coucussū	,, concussū.	
	71	,, B'ingham	,, B'nīgham.	
	76	,, Tisteshal	,, Tifteshal.	
	79	,, Hemford	,, Heinford?	
	82	,, de Saffrei	,, fil' Saffrei.	
	87	,, bodis	,, rodis.	
	90	,, Rocisin	,, Roeisia.	
	90	,, Argentis	,, Argentes.	
	92	,, Leswin	,, Lefwin?	
	96	,, Buistard	,, Buiscard?	
	115	,, Berchenestic	,, Berchenestie?	
	117	,, Beretrevestic	,, Beretrenestie?	

Pedes Finium.

The nature of the Feet of Fines, notes of some of the earlier of which are appended to this paper, is I think so well known as not to warrant any lengthened remarks about it from me.

Proved by experience to be the most binding, as well as the most convenient, form of transfer of land that could be devised, these fines (which were nominally an amicable arrangement, putting an end to a hostile suit in the King's Court) became most deservedly popular with the public, not only from their efficacy, but from the safety ensured to a purchaser by the fact of a duplicate of each fine being preserved of record in the custody of the court.

On their value to the topographer and, to a less degree, to the genealogist, I need not dilate, though I may remind my readers that the earlier fines give minute accounts of the transfer of advowsons, manors, &c., at a date when deeds are excessively rare.

To the antiquary who is neither genealogist nor topographer they will be of less interest, unless to the ethnologist, to whom the overwhelming proportion of Saxon and Danish in comparison with the Norman names, may seem to bear out the opinion that the Normans were numerically but a handful among the people they conquered, and to whom the many curious names of fields and localities, long since forgotten, may prove useful as rough material for his consideration.

Occasionally, however, we find in them entries interesting for other reasons. Thus Humphry de Herlham in 8 Ric. I. sold, for a hundred shillings, land to Ralph de Herlham (possibly his brother) for his equipment to Jerusalem, probably in the fifth Crusade then being instituted by Pope Innocent III.; and the objection naturally felt by large landowners to their sub-tenants giving land into mortmain is well instanced by Eva daughter of Hawis de Morlai granting lands to Ralph de Torcy and his assigns—"præter quam viris religiosis."

The nominal considerations for the grants are sometimes noteworthy—as, a pair of white gloves, a pair of spurs, a pound of cinnamon, and a pound of pepper or sixpence.

A few words on the Feet of Fines themselves may not be inappropriate. They are written in a very small writing on pieces of parchment about as long as, but narrower than one's hand, indented or notched along the top, and are as a rule in good condition.

From the following exact transcript of one of them a better idea of their form and contractions may be gleaned than from any description however ample.

H ⸓ final 9cord fc͞a In Cur͞ D͞ni Reg̃ ap̃ Norwic͞ Anno Regni R̝ Ric͞ vij° Die Sabb festo S͞c͞o Mar͞g Cora͞ Will de Glāvill ꝛ Osb fil Huic͞ ꝛ Sim͞ de Patesh Justic͞ D͞ni Reg̃ ꝛ Alijs fidelib; D͞ni Reg̃ ꝛc ibid p͞sentib; In͞t Rob de Hicford pet͞ ꝛ Adā de Nereford teū de . viij . acr͞ c͞ pti͞n ī Spham . uñ assa' de morte añcessoris su˚mo͞n fuit In͞t eos ī cur͞ p͞fata: Scilt qd id̃ Adā cōcessit cid̃ Rob ꝛ hedib⁹ suis totā p͞dcām t͞rā) cū pti͞n tenend de se ꝛ hēdib; suis ⸓ Reddendo In͞ añuati sex denar͞ ad fest' S͞ci Mich . ꝛ ad xx . sol de Scutag̃ : vi d̃ ꝛ ad plus ⸓ plus . ꝛ ad min⁹ ⸓ min⁹ p ōi 9suetudine : ꝛ p h͞a cōcessone id̃ Rob ded' dc͞o Ade tria Bizantia

Norf⁹

The above extended reads thus—

Hec est finalis concordia facta in curia Domini Regis apud Norwicum anno regni Regis Ricardi septimo die Sabbati festo Sancte Margarete Coram Willelmo de Glanvill et Osberto filio Hervici et Simone de Pateshill Justiciariis Domini Regis et aliis fidelibus Domini Regis &c. ibidem presentibus Inter Robertum de Hickford petentem et Adam de Nereford tenentem de 8 acris cum pertinentibus in Sparham. Unde Assisa de morte antecessoris summonita fuit inter eos in curia prefata; scilicet quod idem Adam concessit eidem Roberti et heredibus suis totam predictam terram cum pertinentibus Tenendum de se et heredibus suis Reddendo inde annuatim sex denarios ad festum Sancti Michaelis et ad 20 solidos de scutagio sex denarios et ad plus plus et ad minus minus pro omni consuetudine Et pro hac concessione idem Robertus dedit dicto Ade tria bizantia.

     Norfolchia.

And translated, thus—

This is the final agreement made in the Court of (our) Lord the King at Norwich on the Sabbath day, in the feast of St. Margaret, in the 7th year of King Richard, before William de Glanvill, Osbert Fitz Hervey, and Simon de Pateshill, Justices of (our) Lord the King, and other faithful (servants) of (our) Lord the King, &c., there present, between Robert de Hickford (the) demandant, and Adam de Nereford (the) tenant of eight acres with (their) appurtenances in Sparham, concerning which an assize of mort d'auncestor was summoned between them in the aforesaid court.

Namely, that the said Adam granted to the said Robert and his heirs all the aforesaid land with (its) appurtenances. To hold of him and his heirs, paying therefor yearly sixpence, and for every twenty shillings of scutage sixpence, and for more more and for less less, for all service.

And the said Robert for this grant gives to the said Adam three bezants.

Norfolk.

None of the Fines for Norfolk have been printed except in the experiment mentioned hereafter.

The volumes published by the Record Commission in 1835—44 under the title of "Fines sive Pedes Finium," reach only to Beds, Bucks, and a few other counties whose initial letters rejoice in an early place in the alphabet.

Nor, from their commencement until the 1st Henry VIII., are there any indexes whatever to them.[1] Anterior to the last-named date the fines themselves[2] must be searched.

From the 25th Henry VIII., however, the *Index to* (the Notes or duplicates of) *the Fines*, which gives short notices of the fines of each term arranged under the counties to which they belong, becomes available.

Up to the 32nd George II. these indices give the Christian names of the parties, and the name of the locality as well.

From the 1st George III., however, the entries run thus—

Bell | Townley | Millet

Millett being the attorney's name. These indices being, though not alphabetical, easy to search, are of course very valuable.

---

[1] There certainly are a few (eleven) volumes purporting to be indices to fines which have been noted by private collectors, chiefly Le Neve, but these refer to so infinitesimally small a portion of the fines that they are perfectly useless. Some counties it is true have separate indices to some of their fines, but Norfolk is unluckily not so blessed.

[2] Which are bound up in thin bundles or parts of twenty-five.

The Books of Entries of Fines, which extend from 1611, are arranged in a similar way to the last-named series, but give a little more information, viz., the entry mentioned above, in them stands thus—

 297. Henry Bell esq Plt & William Townley & Mary his wife & others Defts in Wrettone—Millett.

But the chief use of them is that the late volumes of this series give references to the actual number borne by the Fine.

Lastly, the *King's Silver Books* (which exist from the reign of Henry VIII., but owing to damage done them by fire are inconsultable until that of George I.) give yet more information about the property and parties, *e.g.*, the above referred to entry is thus extended.

 20/. *Norfolk* Henry Bell Esqre Plt Wm Townley & 13/4
 8 St Hil Robt Thorpe & Ann Mary his wife
    defts of 2 mess 1 barn 1 sta 2 cur
    2 gar 1 or 20 La 20 mea 20 pas &
    com of pass for all mann of catt with
    the app^{ts} in Wretton & Stoke ffery
    Bfore Harvey Goodwin & Jno Houchen
    gents by com̄ 29 Decr 38 K Geo 3

Other ways of getting references to fines there are, as by searching the "Covenant Book" and the "Concords of Fines," but as they are generally more troublesome to find, and give less satisfactory information when found, I think the three series above detailed will suffice for the amateur genealogist.

With a few words on an undertaking relative to these fines which was some time ago commenced by our Society, I will conclude.

It was originally intended to print these fines at length; in fact sixteen pages of them, containing extended copies and English précis of the first dozen fines, were printed in 1863, with an able Introduction and equally able Notes, by the Rev. G. H. Dashwood; but owing to the gentleman who supplied copies of such twelve fines failing to send any more, the publication of them has never been continued.

As all the information contained in these fines is capable of being shown in a much more concise and consultable way in a tabular form than by printing them *in extenso*, the former method has been adopted, as by its means more than five times the quantity of information can be given in the same space than by the latter.

WALTER RYE.

Chelsea.

Note.—The party before whose name a star (*) is placed is in each case the Grantor—or technically he who "quits claim."

PEDES FINIUM:

OR

𝔉ines 𝔑elating to the County of 𝔑orfolk.

No.	Date.	"Petens."	"Tenens."
1	3 Richard I.	*Robert de Mortuo Mari.	The Prior of Lewwes (by Symon Dean of Hecgham.)
2	7 Richard I.	Avicia daughter of Hamund Tusard (by John de Fric.)	*Roger de Acra and Emma Tusard his wife.
3	—	Robert de Hicford.	*Adam de Nereford.
4	—	*Roger Gulafre and Beatrix his wife.	Robert son of Symon de Saham.
5	—	*Lecelina and Beatrix, daughters of Edric.	Gaufridus son of Gervase.
6	—	*Safrid son of William and Botilda his wife.	William de Tikebrom, Robert son of Reginald and Ulfus de Sucinestorp and William his son.
7	—	*Adam son of Achard.	The Monks of Acre and Alan son of Reiner.
8	—	*William Picot.	William de Anemere.
9	—	*Nicholas Pincerna.	Ralph abbot of Hulm̄ (by John the monk.)
10	—	Wlvive, Botilda, and Levive.	*William Spine.
11	—	Bartholomew son of Gaufridus.	*Reginald de Camera.
12	—	Ralph de Lenham.	*Henry de Matham.
13	—	*Jocelin son of Ralph.	Richard son of Elebald.
14	—	*William son of Ralph.	William and Fulco the sons of Evis.

Description of Property.	Consideration, &c.
One fourth part of a Knight's fee in Heegham. (†) All land held by the said Prior of the said Robert, in Tomestuñ and Cattestuñ, of the yearly value of 10 shillings and of 8 pence respectively.	The annual payment of 6 marks of silver and the release of (†)
60 acres in Tiringtoñ.	The regrant of the western moiety of the said premises to the said Avicia, at the yearly rent of 4ˢ 4ᵈ.
8 acres in Sperham.	3 bezants, the yearly rent of 6ᵈ, and 6ᵈ for every 20ˢ of scutage.
A mill in Glosebreg̃.	5 marks of silver to Roger and 2 bezants to Beatrix; and the annual rent of 10ˢ.
Two acres in Nesse.	10ˢ sterling.
10 acres in Sweinestorp.	One mark of silver and a heifer worth 32ᵈ.
40 acres in Feltewell.	2½ marks of silver.
30 acres in Wulferton, namely all that Roger, father of the said William de Anemere, held there. To hold for the life of Christiana the mother of the said William de Anemere.	The yearly rent during the life of the said Christiana of 40ˢ.
The advowson of the Church of North Walesham.	3 marks of silver.
12 acres in Northtoñ.	The profits thereof during the same year.
11 acres in Cree. (†) 3 acres of the same land, viz., 1½ rod at the head of the croft of Robert son of Scule, 3 rods at Sorteland, 2 rods and "unam midfurlongam dimidiam acram" in Hartesdal, and 3 rods in Hameldon,	The grant by Bartholomew to the said Reginald and to Ralph his son of (†)
40ˢ rent in Dallig̃ and in Toring̃.	at the yearly rent of 9ᵈ.
(†) £4 rent in Egleston.	30 marks of silver and the grant of (†)
4 acres in Carleton.	7ˢ sterling.
20 acres in Wicingesete	The regrant of one fourth of said land at the service due therefor, viz., 15ᵈ.

No.	Date.	"Petens."	"Tenens."
15	7 Ric. I.	*Acelina de Stāfield and Reginald de Stāfield her nephew.	Richard p̄p̄osit of Doketon.
16	—	*Roger Le Norreis.	Hugh son of Elinne.
17	—	*Goldrūn daughter of Offing.	Eustace de Sireford.
18	—	Walter son of Galfridus.	*John, capellanus of Tunstal.
19	—	*William son of Scule.	Hardwin son of Haldein and Simon de Foxhol.
20	—	Richard & Henry the sons of Odo.	*William son of Godard.
21	—	John son of Walter.	*William son of Thurkil.
22	—	William son of Roger and Matilda his wife.	*Saher de Biskele.
23	—	Thomas Le Bigod and Agnes his wife (by Roger de Reppes.)	*Robert de Glanvill.
24	—	*Richard son of H̄lewiñ and Ainalda his wife.	Gaufr⁹ son of Robert, and Godwin son of Ralph
25	—	*William de Curzū.	Robert son of Rocelin.
26	—	*Ailward and Emma his wife, daughter of Eudo.	Peter son of B⁾te (Beatrix?)
27	—	*Walter and Leuric sons of Dering.	Osb. M̄catorē
28	—	Comitissa Gundreda (by Nicholas clericus.)	*William de Stᵃton.
29	—	*Robert le Flittere.	Wigot Mercator.
30	—	Ralph de Lenham.	*William son of Helye.

Description of Property.	Consideration, &c.
10 acres in Dunton.	16^s sterling.
6½ acres in Sireford.	½ a mark of silver.
8 acres in Sireford.	One mark of silver.
1 acre in Tunstal.	5^s of silver and the profits of the land for the aforesaid year.
4 acres in Wichīghā.	One mark of silver.
3 acres in Neuwater.	12^d and the profits of the same land for the aforesaid year.
30 acres in Stanford. (†) 7 acres in Hengham, namely all which he (John) had from the land of Richard de Stanlund, and half an acre in the close of the said John.	The grant from John to William of (†)
2^s rent in Grenesvill.	40^s of silver, the yearly rent of 12^d, and 5^d in the 20^s "ad exercitū dn̄i reg̃."
A carucate of land in Roctoñ.	5 marks.
9 perches of land in Dockinges.	5^s of silver.
One fifth of a knight's fee in Blakewrde.	5 marks of silver and 3^s.
6 acres in Heidon for which the lessors agree to pay a rent of 6^d to their superior landlords.	The annual rent of 21^d.
Messuage in Disce.	6^s sterling.
The advowson of the Church of St. Peter of St^{a}ton to Gundreda for life "ut illi^9 ecc^a q̃ ptinet ad libam̃ dot̄c ipi^9 Gundr̃^{9} et p^{9}t decessū ipi^9 Gundr̃^{9} Comite Rog̃ le bigod ⁊ hedibȝ suis."	60^s sterling.
5 acres in Birston.	10^s sterling.
20 acres in Terning. (†) 10 acres of above property, viz., 5^a which were of William Bemeig and 5^a near the land of Robert Pattarin "versus occidentē ante portā Howard,"	The grant by Ralph to W^m. of (†) at the yearly rent of 2^s.

No.	Date.	"Petens."	"Tenens."
31	7 Richard I.	*Hugh son of Sturmi.	Walter de Elingham.
32	—	Stephen de Rolvesbi (vel Rolnesbi.)	*Richard de Clipesbi.
33	—	*Brialed son of Brūmā.	Ralph son of Bōde and Emma his wife.
34	—	*Godein son of Godwin	Richard son of Sigenild.
35	—	*Robert de Cokefeld (by William clericus.)	Thomas de Hasting.
36	—	*Robert de Mortemer.	John Leestange.
37	—	Roger son of Honfr?	*Helvisa sister of the said Roger.
38	—	Robert son of Simon de Saham.	*Henry de Turnecurt.
39	—	Stephen de Ludinge.	*Robert Le Wile.
40	—	Baldwin de Bures and Imbria his wife.	*Eustace de Ho, the heir of Warin, formerly husband of the said Imbria.

Description of Property.	Consideration, &c.
18 acres in Elingham.	20ˢ sterling.
60 acres in Burg and Clipesbi.	The regrant of same at the yearly rent of 10ˢ.
3ᵃ in Crcic.	20ˢ sterling.
4 acres in Bˡsele (Brisley ?)	7ˢ sterling.
24 acres in Frense, viz., "de feodo Sc̄i Edmundi," and 30 acres in Tistchal, and land which was of Sleuetunge in Gissing, and land which was of Wicescard, and 6 acres of the fee of Roger de Gissing.	6 marks of silver.
5 knights' fees in Hunestaneston, Totington, Ringsted, and Sniterton.	The grant by the said John to the said Robert of (†)
(†) All the land of the said John in Totington at the service of one knight's fee less a twentieth part, (except the church of the same town, which the said John, with the consent of the said Robert, gave to the church of the B. Mary of Kāpess "ij monialibȝ ibidē dō ˢvientibȝ"—and except the service, &c., of Henry de Turnecort in Totinton, of Hvs filᵒ Hugᵒ Leestᵃuge, of John de Kerebroc, of Emma de Mora, of William de Bruna, of the Prior of Tifford, of Malpas, of William son of Simon Faber, and of Wᵐ Leres,)	and the payment by the said John to the said Robert of £100 of silver.
30 acres in Wĭtreton.	The regrant by the said Roger to the said Helvisa of (†)
(†) 9 acres of the same land (named in fine.)	
40 acres in Totington.	20/. & the yearly payment of one pound of pepper or sixpence, & 4ᵈ in the 20/. of the king's scutage.
1 virgate in Uptun.	The regrant by the said Robert of (†)
†) a moiety of the same land.	At the rent of "qn̄dā albas cyrotecas."
Dower of all the lands of Berewic which were of Wulmard Butekarl, in the parish of Riwehall (Runhall ?) and half a mark's rent in the same place, payable by Fulcher de Aldeholt, (2/.) and Goce de Ho (4/8.)	

No.	Date.	"Petens."	"Tenens."
41	8 Richard I.	Robert de Colevill and Alicia his wife.	*Alexander Pointell and Alicia his wife, daughter of the said Alicia de Colevill.
42	—	Thomas son of Michael, (" q^i infra etate est.")	*Eustace de Talcolneston.
43	—	*Alicia ...... and Richard her son.	Deodatus prior of St. Faith of Horsham.
44	—	Elyas Bourami.	*Bartholomew Redham.
45	—	*Alice daughter of Martin.	Ralph de Verli.
46	—	*John de Frid.	Peter de Frid.
47	—	Warin de Salle by Thomas, and Matthew his sons.	*Warin de Ermingland.
48	—	Robert son of Roger.	*William de Reddam son of Mathew.
49	—	John Hautein.	*Prior and monks of St. Mary of Acre (by Mag^r Richeriū de Fuheldon.)
50	—	Simon de Cliketot.	*Nicholas de Walesham.
51	—	Julian de Swathfold.	*William de Corechun.
52	—	Robert clericus de Ructon.	*Adam son of Helye de Sipeden.
53	—	Ralph de Herlhā	*Umfridus de Herlhā.

Description of Property.	Consideration, &c.
One third part of Metton, as dower from the gift of William de Nevill, her late husband.	The annual sum of 3 marks of silver.
30 acres in Talcolneston.	(none)
......acres in Alingeton.	Annual rent of 6ᵈ.
50 acres in Nortun.	10 marks of silver and half a mark annual rent.
Half a knight's fee in Hulm and Snetesham.	The grant by the said Ralph to the said Alice of (†)
(†) 14 acres in Snetesham and 3/. of yearly rent in the same town which John Le Moinne held.	at the yearly rent of 6ᵈ.
24 acres in Tilence.	The payment of 20/. sterling and grant by Peter to John, of (†)
(†) 16 acres called Gittiscroft between the land of Ade Tholl and Peter de Frid, also 3 acres called Geggiscroft, where the capital messuage of the said John de Frid is,	At the yearly rent of 12ᵈ.
24 acres in Corpesti.	At the yearly rent of 3ˢ. and 2ᵈ.
(†) 2 acres "in Westig̃ med de Corpesti."	The grant by Warin de Salle to W. de Ermingland of (†)
Advowson of the Church of Lippenhoe.	15 marks of silver.
Advowson of Hailesdon (?) and the tithes of the mills of the same town and land called Rutligehal.	The grant in exchange to the prior by the said John of (†)
(†) The Church of Heringby, which however Robert Hautein, brother of the said John, was to hold for his life, paying to the same monks 20/. a year nomine pensionis.	
"De ultima rep̃sentacõe ecclie Sc̃e marie de Walesham."	"unū ostur̃ sor." [A hawk of the first year.]
1½ knight's fee in Helmingham.	30 marks of silver.
34 acres in Sipeden and half the service of Roger Clericus, and half the service of Reginald Palmer.	40ˢ of silver and the yearly service of 47½ᵈ.
A carucate of land in Herlhã, (except the mill of Herlhã for life of Humphrey.)	The grant to Muriild the daughter of the said Humphrey of (†)
(†) 20 acres in Hlhã.	at the rent of 6ᵈ. yearly.

No.	Date.	"Petens."	"Tenens."
54	8 Richard I.	*William son of Walter.	William son of Eudo.
55	—	John de Sarenton.	*Robert Dinat.
56	—	Peter son of Galfridus.	*Eudo de Racheia and Galfr and Simon his brothers.
57	—	*Hardwin de Wareñe and Christiana his wife and William Faber of Wichingham and Mabill his wife.	William Batallie.
58	—	Alan son of Richard.	*Roger son of Tome (Thomas ?)
59	—	John Le Moine in the place of Margaret his sister.	*Roger Buche
60	—	*Reginald son of Torrond.	Richard Capell of Mouton (by William Freman his attorney.)
61	—	*Peter son of Richard de Wiggenhal.	William son of Alan de Clenchewarton.

Description of Property.	Consideration, &c.
	For which Ralph gave to the said Humfrey 100/. "ad peg'inaconē suā faciend ad Jerlm."
½ a carucate of land in E. and W. Tudchā. (†) 37½ acres, viz., 4½ which Robert Sturel holds, 3 which William Godsaule holds, 3½ in Estcroft, and 24 which lie between the church of Tudchā "et divisa de Alsinges," and 2½ which Alice fil' Aki holds in E. Tudchā, and ⅙th part of the mill of Gladeware, at the yearly rent of 6/., scutage, &c.	The grant (in exchange) by W^m. fil' Eudo to W^m. fil' Walter of (†)
	For which W^m. fil' Walter pays 5 marks of silver.
40 acres in Sarenton, formerly of Swani, father of the said John.	The grant of (†)
(†) One of above acres situate in Hethincroft.	For which Robert pays 40/. sterling and 2^d a year.
Advowson of Racheia.	40/.
20 acres in Sueineton and lands that were of Gaufr⁹ fil Wider.	1 mark of silver to Hardwin and wife, 13^s sterling to Faber and wife, and a grant to Hardwin and wife of (†)
(†) 2 acres in Sueineton, viz., 3 rods in Barlicroft, 1 acre in Nordinge, and one rod formerly of Robert Eive.	To hold at the yearly rent of 6^d.
Land in Litleholm.	The grant in exchange to Roger of (†)
(†) 3 acres in Draeton, 1 acre in Caldewell, 4 acres "in occidente ptē vie de Binnā," 2 pieces of land at Witemedes, and 2 acres at Merslades,	at the yearly rent of 18^d, and 3^d for every 20/. of scutage. Alan also pays 8 marks of silver.
One knight's fee in Walton, to hold to the Abbot, &c., of the Premonasterian order of Derham.	50 marks of silver paid by the said Abbot to Roger, and 50 to John.
Two acres in Mouton, to hold to Lucent, Jacob and Roger, sons of the said Reginald, by the consent of the said Richard.	1 mark of silver and the yearly rent of 4^d.
4 ploughlands in Clenchewarton, Wygenhal, Tilnei, Islington, Lenn, and Grimeston,	

c

No.	Date.	"Petens."	"Tenens."
62	8 Richard I.	Roger Le Eu.	*Adam son of Gilbert de Elcham.
63	—	Roger de Brom.	William de Pirnho.
64	—	Sansoñe Abbot of St. Edmund.	Alexander son of Gobol de Kirechbi.
65	—	*Hawis daughter of Henry de Shireford.	William de Creic.
66	—	*Amicia.	Ralph de Verli.
67	—	*William and Roger de Sudfeld.	Ralph abbot of St. Benedict of Holme.
68	—	*Richard de Lechesham.	William de Huntingefeld and Isabel his wife (by William their attorney.)
69	—	*Roger Picot.	Deodatus prior of the Church of St. Faiths of Horsham.
70	9 Richard I.	Hugo clericus.	*Richard son of Stephen.

Description of Property.	Consideration, &c.
which the said William held of the fee of Simon fil' Richard and Ernald de Torlee, and Peter de Bekeswell, and St. Eadmund, and St. Etheldreth, and St. Pancratius, and Robert de Cap^avill, and Godfrey de Lisewis, and the Count of Brittannie, and the Earl of Clare, and the Prior of Westacre.	
(†) All the tenements which Richard the father of the said Peter, held in Wiggēhall, of the said William the day he died, viz., 10 acres in Tilnei, called Pottescroft, 15 acres formerly of Sibilia de Tilnei, abutting towards the south on the croft of Ralph de Hauvill, (at the service of a quarter of a knight's fee) and all the land of Grimeston, which belonged to the said William in the same town, at	The grant in exchange to the said Peter of (†)
20 acres in Elēham, (Ellingham?)	The yearly rent of 22^s. 2 marks of silver.
A mill in Pirnho.	
One knight's fee in Kirechbi, (Kirby.)	The acquittance of all arrears.
26 acres in Creic, (Creake.)	20 shillings sterling.
Land which was of Cecilie de Humē, (Holme) mother of the said Ralph de Verli in Humē and Snetesham.	2½ marks of silver.
Advowson of the Church of St. Peter of Reppes and advowson of Ashebi.	The grant in exchange of (†)
(†) Land called Fouracres in campo de Sudfeld, (Suffeld.)	
60 acres in Lechesham, (Lexham) "et totam brueriam (*brushwood*) de chemino de Norton usque Harthornesgate.	The grant in exchange of (†)
(†) 20 acres in Lucham (Lytcham,) 30 acres in Quenhill, 2 acres in the same town, and 4 acres of brushwood, "que tangunt caput novi *frussati* ejusdem Willelmi."	
12 acres in Colneia.	5^s sterling.
9 acres in Osmundeston.	The grant in exchange of (†)
(†) 3 rods lying before the gate of the said Richard, at	1^d a year rent.

No.	Date.	"Petens."	"Tenens."
71	9 Richard I.	*Nicholas son of Hugo.	Magister Simon de Tornham.
72	—	Warin de Saulle (by Thomas and Matthew his sons.)	*Philip capellanus de Saulle.
73	—	William de Len and Simon his brother.	*Ivo.
74	—	*Blakewin de Thornham.	Goscelin Feutrarius.
75	—	Walter de Basingham.	*William Flemang and Matilda de Besevill.
76	—	Geoffrey son of Walter.	*Bernard son of Durand.
77	—	Peter son of Richard.	*John son of Alan de Reinham.
78	—	Warin de Saule (by Thomas and Matthew his sons.)	*John capellanus of Corpeste.
79	—	*Richard de Becco (by William de Becco.)	William de Hasting.
80	—	*Alan de Mundeham.	Peter de Egelfeld (by Henry de Brō.)
81	10 Richard I.	William de Bee and Hugo clericus.	*Roger son of Pagan.

Description of Property.	Consideration, &c.
	"Et pro p̄dcis iij rodis terre id̄ Ric̄ devenit homo ip̄s Hugonis."
A ploughland in Tornham, (Thornham.)	The regrant of (†)
(†) 10 acres of the same land which D^{ns} Robert Batevill held lying in Tikewell, (Tytchwell) and Turnham.	
20 acres in Saulle (Salle) and Ilinetone (Illington?)	The regrant to Philip for his life of (†)
(†) Two parts of the same land,	at the yearly rent of 9^d and two capons.
Half a messuage in Lynn.	5 marks of silver.
A messuage in Lynn.	12 marks of silver.
Half a knight's fee in Matlask.	60 marks of silver and the yearly rent of......
7 acres in Tacolneston.	5^s.
One knight's fee in Grimeston.	The regrant of (†)
(†) half of the same land besides the capital messuage.	To hold of John at the service of a pair of "calcariū de auratoz de p̄cio vj denar̄" (gilt spurs worth 6^d.)
	Peter pays to John 10 marks of silver.
20 acres in Corpeste (Corpusty.)	The lease of the same land to the said John for his life at 2^s 6^d yearly.
	And that Warin "quietabit idem Johañem contra Prior̄ et Convēn de S̄ca Fide."
100^s rent in ...... of which Richard quits claim against William "ex dono Henrici frat's sui cui9 cartā ht."	30 marks of silver.
Half a knight's fee in Mundham for 15 years.	24 marks of silver and the rent as to 9 acres of a pound of "cinimi" (? cinnamon.)
8 acres in Wode Dallinges—4 acres whereof to be free alms to the church of Dalling, viz., 1 acre called Sternelond, 1 called Sandlond, 3 rods in Estecroft, 3 rods in Milneland, ½ acre at Iscris.	The grant to Ralph capellanus, brother of the said Roger, of the same 4 acres for life at 20^d rent.

No.	Date.	"Petens."	"Tenens."
82	10 Richard I.	....	....
83	—	*Vincent son of Alan and Robert his brother.	Henry son of Bruinsewein and Roger and Richard his brothers.
84	—	*William de Arden and Isolda his wife.	William de Fossato.
85	—	Reginald son of Hervey.	*Alan filius Presbiteri and Helewis his wife.
86	—	*Ralph de Boilund.	Ranulph son of Robert de Stratun.
87	—	*Hodierna daughter of Aluric de Rudham.	Hervey the prior and the Convent of St. Mary of Rudham.
88	—	*Ivo son of Brunsewein.	William son of Stangrun.
89	—	*Joseph son of Alcluri (?)	William Wudecok.
90	—	*Thomas son of Adam.	Lecelina de g̃neɱ (Yarmouth?) and William her son.
91	—	*Roger son of Thurstan.	Humphry son of Ralph.
92	—	*Hermer son of John.	William son of Augustin.
93	—	*William son of Wido.	Peter de Holcham.
94	—	*Thurketell son of Edwin.	Richard Orgar, Claricia who was the wife of Humfrey, Swarin son of Osbert, and Matilda and Agnes his sisters.

Description of Property.	Consideration, &c.
And the said Roger also gives to the said church a pasture in Kirbemor. (Illegible—relates to property in Lodne granted to the Prior of ……) 9 acres in Sadelboge.	One mark of silver.
Land in Adthelbure, Hellingeham, and Bestorp. (†) Land in Wrogiland, and half an acre next to the windmill of Ralph de Burg, 1½ acre at Langedonohavetlond *(sic)* 12½ acres in Langedon Brembelond, land in Brakenholm and Langedon, 3 parcels of land in Gremeston (Grimston.)	The grant in exchange of (†) at the yearly rent of 5/. 12ᵈ.
12 acres in Stratton.	Half a mark of silver and yearly rent of 6ᵈ, and 6ᵈ for every 20ˢ of scutage.
3 acres in Rudham.	10ˢ sterling.
17 acres in Tillene (Tylney.) (†) 2 acres in Gavelefurlinges.	The grant in exchange of (†) at the yearly rent of 6ᵈ.
40 acres in Telvetune (Thelveton.) (†) Half the same land.	The grant to Warin son of the said Joseph of (†) at 32¼ᵈ yearly.
7 messuages in gnem (Yarmouth) and a carucate of land in Blafeld (Blofield.)	10 marks of silver and 6ˢ yearly rent.
1 acre in Berlingham (Burlingham.)	Yearly rent of 1ᵈ.
30 acres in Tuttington. (†) 20 acres in Banningham (except 5 acres which Hermer regrants to William at 4ᵈ rent.)	The release to Hermer of (†)
"De 13 nummatis redditus" in Burnham.	1 mark of silver.
3½ acres in Martham.	½ a mark of silver.

No.	Date.	"Petens."	"Tenens."
95	10 Richard I.	Roger de Cardeston.	*Milo de Nucers.
96	—	*Hervey son of Eund.	Ralph Quarter.
97	—	*Robert son of Waren.	Hugh his brother.
98	—	*Peter and Muriel his wife.	Hakun de Herlham.
99	—	*Emma daughter of Osbert.	Ralph de Bretham.
100	—	*Roger nephew of Harvey.	Simon son of Robert and Geoffrey le Neuman.
101	—	*Goscelin son of Wulnod.	Roger son of Britrich.
102	—	*Thomas de Walecot.	Richd de Runhal.
103	—	*Amelia daughter of Ulf de Limia.	Ralph de Tilencia and Gouti^y le Cupe.
104	—	*Reiner son of Goscelin.	Edward son of Leve.
105	—	*Nicholas son of Reginald.	Richard de Clipesbi.
106	—	*William Faber.	Bartholomew de Cinci.

Description of Property.	Consideration, &c.
Common of pasture in Swaneton.	That Roger and his heirs should have "unū pullū equū unoqoq̨, t'cio anno p manū p̄dci Milonis" and his heirs of the same pasture. In default Peter de Meauton or his heirs are to deliver the first-named animal.
30 acres in Heinford (Haynford?)	1 mark of silver and the regrant to Hervey of (†)
(†) 29 acres of the same land to hold of Wm. Fitz Roscelin at 3ˢ 1ᵈ yearly service.	
...... in Rokelund (Rockland.)	The grant in exchange of (†)
(†) 1 acre at Rokelund at 4ᵈ rent.	
A messuage in Midelton.	The grant in exchange of (†)
(†) 7 acres and a messuage, viz., 2½ in the croft of Wido, 2 in Hiringeshal, and 2½ in Brith.	at 6ᵈ yearly and 2ᵈ for every 20ˢ of scutage.
11 acres in Bagetorp.	20ˢ sterling.
10 acres in Oueltane (Oulton.)	4ˢ sterling and the grant in exchange of (†)
(†) 4 acres in Oueltane.	
16 acres in Len.	The grant in exchange of (†)
(†) 10½ acres, and 1½ acre, and 2 acres and 1 perch in Crosholm, "in pʳto de Len," and ½ acre in the croft of Roger Barat, and 3½ acres in Linecroft, and 2½ acres "in campo de Hech," and 1 acre in Niewcholm.	
2 acres in Birlingham scil. Bremestoft. To hold to the church of St. Andrew of Berlingham, and the said Richard and his heirs and successors.	1 mark of silver.
2 messuages in Lenn de feudo filorū Simonis de Jernemue.	23ˢ 4ᵈ.
30 acres in Duntune.	The regrant of (†)
(†) 6 acres of the same land and 1 acre 1 rod in Sidesternesti, and 3½ perches at Suineswöig, ½ acre in Weistdele, 1 acre in Creiegate, 1 acre in Hudiscroft, ½ acre in Hocee, and 1 acre at Suinesdele,	at the yearly rent of 4¼ᵈ.
30 acres in Clipesbi.	20 marks of silver.
40 acres in Wichingeham (Witchingham.)	1 mark of silver and 9 acres of land in Wichingham at 3ˢ a year.

No.	Date.	"Petens."	"Tenens."
107	10 Richard I.	*Hawis son of Leneve (or Leveve.)	Robert son of Hugh.
108	—	*Henry son of Thurold.	Reiner de Len.
109	—	Thomas son of William.	*Bela, by William her son.
110	—	*Henry son of Gocelin.	Wido son of Roger.
111	—	*Ralph son of Robert.	Ralph son of Ralph, and William son of Adam de Hengam.
112	—	*Alan son of William.	Adam Sacerdos.
113	—	*Alan son of William.	Robert son of Adam and Beatrix his wife.
114	—	*Simon son of Walter.	Hamo son of Nicholas.
115	—	*Richard son of Ketell.	Hugh son of Wlveve.
116	—	Hervey and Huctred.	*Roger son of William.
117	—	*Cuti (?) Bludū.	Estmund Pic.
118	—	*Edwin de Bebrege.	Hardewin son of Ulf.
119	—	*Lambert son of Cohen.	Simon de Maudebi.
120	—	*Robert son of Wlliam.	John son of Wymer (?), John son of Richard, Peter son of Ralph, and Eudo de Stowe.
121	—	*William son of Reginald.	Ædwin fil' Aildivi.

27

Description of Property.	Consideration, &c.
35 acres in Heilesdon.	13ˢ sterling.
5 acres in Len.	2 marks of silver.
11 acres in Frenges.	10ˢ sterling and 9ᵈ a year.
¼ a knight's fee in Meringetorp (Morningthorp.)	40ˢ sterling.
8ˢ and 12ᵈ rent in Ielverton (Yelverton.)	20ˢ sterling (paid by Ralph Fitz Robert.)
"Et p̃dco Rađ fil Rob remanet c̃ˢ sol reddito residur c̃ ptin de cadẽ t̃ra tenẽdi de p̃dco Rađ fil Rađ ̃t hedibe suis ille et hẽdes sui p ˜svic ix den̄ ad xx sol de scutat̃ et ad plus plus et ad minus minus ̃t duoƺ madladoƺ reddidoƺ ad Natal."	
15 acres at Norwalesham.	The grant in exchange of (†)
(†) 1 acre at Walesham at 2ᵈ a year.	
19 acres in Walesham	The regrant of (†)
(†) 4 acres thereof scil. 2 acres (abutting) upon a croft, and 2 acres in Grisetoft, at	6ᵈ yearly.
4 acres in Gatelee.	10ˢ.
18 acres in Horsted.	1 mark of silver.
12 acres and a messuage which were of Ilfred's manor, Wiltun, (Wilton?)	
The grant thereof by Hervey and Huctred to Ralph de Tymelwurde of Hervey and Huctred at 10ˢ rent, and Ralph grants same to Roger son of William for the latter's life at 1ᵈ a year, remainder to Muriel the wife of Roger for her life at same rent, and pays 10ˢ sterling.	
1 messuage in Welles.	20ˢ sterling.
5 acres in Wichingham.	The yearly rent of 17¼ᵈ and the regrant of (†)
(†) 2 acres of the same land and 1 acre "de conquestu suo."	
15 acres in Maudebi.	1 mark of silver.
4 acres in Stowe.	22 shillings sterling.
4 acres in Raugham (? Rougham) to hold to Ædwin for life, after his death William to have one half, and Susanna the daughter of Ædwin the other, she paying to the said William, 8ᵈ yearly.	The grant to the said William of (†)

No.	Date.	"Petens."	"Tenens."
122	10 Richard I.	*Richard son of Robert.	Hugh son of Robert de Witton.
123	—	*Frari son of William.	William de Bello monte.
124	—	*Eva daughter of Hawis de Merlai.	Ralph de Torcy.
125	—	David Hirst and Alice his wife, and Michael and Emma his wife.	*Milo the son of Roger and Matilda his wife.
126	—	*Ailward de Birligh[am] and Edwin his son.	Gilbert de Lingwode and Richard his son.
127	—	*William de Hindringham, by John his brother.	Ralph Prior of Binham.
128	—	*Richard de Geely, Andrew, and Henry.	Hamond Buhurd.
129	—	*Hervey son of William.	Peter de Fritū.
130	—	Robert Coē son of Asalac.	*William fil' Ade.
131	—	Alan de Loph[am].	*Hugh de Heia.

Description of Property.	Consideration, &c.
(†) The capital messuage of the said land and a rod and a half of land in exchange for half an acre at Estgate.	
4 acres in Witton.	2 marks of silver.
½ an acre in Hacford.	The grant in exchange of (†)
(†) ½ acre in Sevenacris, which Reginald son of Richard held.	
40 acres in Hillingeton, and a mill called Vuermilne, (overmill?) to hold "predicto Radulfo et cuicumq̃ illam dedit vel assignavit præter quam viris relligiosis."	100^s sterling and the yearly rent of 9^s 8^d.
46 acres in Sueinestorp.	1 mark of silver and the regrant of two-thirds of premises for the life of Matilda at the yearly rent of 6^s.
1½ acre in Lingwode.	The regrant of half the said land situate in campis de Lingwode, viz., 1½ rods in Brodeland, and 1½ rod in the 8 acre (field) to hold at the yearly service of 2^d.
30 acres in Bernai.	10 marks of silver.
60 acres in Horingetoft and Witigsete (Whissonsett.)	12 marks of silver, for 20^s part whereof Alice, the mother of the said Richard, Andrew, and Henry, quits claim of her dower in said premises.
14^a in Tutēn (Tuttington).	The regrant by Peter to his brother Hervey of 6 acres thereof (?) [This fine is very faded and almost illegible.]
5^a in Kikeligton.	The regrant of part of said land.
10^a in Lopham.	Half a mark, and the regrant of same to Hugh at the yearly rent service of 20 marks.

No.	Date.	"Petens."	"Tenens."
132	10 Richard I.	*Alice daughter of Roger Faber.	Reginald Faber.
133	—	*Eustace Falconar.	Thomas son of Simon.
134	—	*John son of Osbert.	Thurstan son of Wluricus.
135	—	Simon de Warenn and Alveva his wife.	Richard son of Fulcher, and Andrew son of Harvy, and Nicholas son of Robert.
136	—	Roger de Ratlesden.	*Gocelin de Birlingham and Matilda his wife.
137	—	*Simon de Warenn and Alveva his wife.	Bernard p^mm and Wictieve de Hoewood.
138	—	Emma dau. of Avant (?)	*Roger son of Runilda.
139	—	*Godwin fil' Leffi.	Henry nephew of Turild.
140	—	William Rolland and Alice his wife.	Bartholomew and (*) Godefrey Galt.
141	—	*Herbert son of Odo.	Richard parson of Reindon.
142	—	Gaufridus son of Turketel.	*Godard son of Alveva, and Reginald, and William, and John, and Osegod, sons of Godard.
143	—	*Randulfus and John.	Adam de Herdwic.
144	—	Ulf son of Asketel.	*William Kinesmā[n].
145	—	*Hervey Faber.	Richard clericus de Brētham.
146	—	Thomas son of William.	*Aloesius de Frenḡ.

Description of Property.	Consideration, &c.
5ᵃ in Wigenhal.	The regrant to Alice of all her land towards the south thereof lying between her house and the water of Wigenhal aforesaid, to hold of the capital lord of the fee at the service of 1ᵈ.
140ᵃ in the marsh of Claia.	The regrant to Eustace of 40ᵃ and of 9ᵃ which Boidinsot held, at 16ˢ a year.
3ᵃ in Wigenhal.	Half a mark of silver.
10ᵃ and 1 toft in Feltwell.	The grant to Helias son of Philip and his heirs of half the said property to hold of Simon and wife at 6ᵈ yearly.
A third part of the advowson of Bucke[n]ham.	13 marks of silver.
4ᵃ and one messuage in Hocwood (Hockwold.)	The grant to Simon of 1 acre "juxta Witegate" to hold at 3ᵈ yearly.
Half of 16ᵃ in Witton.	The quit-claim by Emma to Roger of the other moiety.
10ᵃ in Tirinton.	40ˢ and 3 sheep.
⅓ an acre and ½ a rood in Karsť (Caistor ?)	12ᵈ paid by William and Alice, and the regrant thereof at 2ᵈ yearly rent.
7ᵃ in Ridon *(sic)* to hold to Roger son of the said Richard.	4ˢ paid by Roger to Herbert.
10ᵃ in West Weni (West Winch ?)	3 marks of silver, &c.
8ᵃ in Herdwic, to hold of Randulf and John, at the yearly rent of 12ᵈ.	20ˢ.
3½ acres in Derham.	The regrant to William of half the said land, and the payment to Ulf of half a mark.
6ᵃ in Bretham (Brentham ?)	⅓ a mark of silver.
10 acres in Frenḡ.	20ˢ of silver.

No.	Date.	"Petens."	"Tenens."
147	10 Richard I.	*Reginald son of Roger and Beatrix his wife, and Beatrix sister of the said Beatrix, daughters of Roger.	William de Wudington.
148	—	William de Gurnai.	*Martin de Wertlai.
149	—	*Reiner son of Osbert and Ailleth his wife, and Roger Qrter and Engelieth his wife.	Henry son of Brumswein.
150	—	*Hawis fil' Stang'm.	William son of John de Wauton.
151	—	*Hawis daughter of Geoffrey Lance.	Henry de Bolewic.
152	—	*Richard son of Ourverd.	Wimer de Cantele.
153	—	*Baldehiva daughter of William son of Adelstan de Hechingham.	William de Rochahe.
154	—	*Emma daughter of Robert.	Stephen Spurcat.

Description of Property.	Consideration, &c.
10 acres in Tistleshall.	The release by William of all his interest in 6 acres in the fields of Tistleshall, which Alviva vidua held of Abbot of St. Edmond's at 12^d yearly, and the payment by William to Beatrix the wife of Reginald of 2 marks, and to Beatrix her sister of ... shillings, a mantle, and a tunic.
1½ acre in Burnham, to hold of Martin at 12^d yearly.	10^s.
4 acres and 2 parts of half a messuage in Wigenhale.	8^s sterling.
12 acres in Wauton (Wooton ?)	The regrant by William to Hermer his son and the son of the said Hawis of half the said land at 10^d yearly.
5 acres, part of 6 acres in Heveringeland.	The regrant by Henry of 1^a thereof lying to the east, and the payment by Henry of 20^s.
12 acres in Cantele.	The regrant of 1½ acre and 1 rod part thereof, to hold of Wimer at 9^d yearly rent.
15 acres in Hechingham.	3½ marks.
56 acres in Mendham. (†) 18^a in Mendham versus Norfolc, and $5\frac{1}{4}^a$ "inter feod Thō de Mendham Bñdcti decani," and $4\frac{1}{2}^a$ and a rod and 3 rods between the lauds "Precentoris Lond et Thō de Mendham," and 1^a 1^{rod} between the land of Geoffrey Parson and the land of the Precentor, and $2\frac{1}{4}^a$ between the fee of Tho. de Mendham and Humphrey Faber, and 1ª between the fee of Tho. de Mendham and Humphrey fil. Robert, and 1^a in Udostoft, and 1½ acre "ante portā Steph Spurcat."	The grant of (†) at the yearly rent of 3^s 8^d, and 4^d the 20^s of scutage; Stephen also pays Emma 20^s.

No.	Date.	"Petens."	"Tenens."
155	10 Richard I.	*Hugh son of Roger.	Robert Brien.
156	—	*Godwin son of Gosse.	Richard son of Sigar.
157	—	Bartholomew son of Edric.	*Bartholomew de Ægefeld.
158	—	Hugh de Ranis.	*Bartholomew de Ægefeld.
159	—	*William son of Scule.	Houward Lomb and Herman his son.
160	—	Other son of Elwin.	*Reginald son of Thorad.
161	—	*Ralph son of Reginald.	Helias le Colnere.
162	—	Richard son of Walter.	*Robert Buinard.
163	—	*Eustace de Bavent.	Richard son of Nicholas.
164	—	Avicia daughter of Henry.	*Thomas Hautein.
165	—	*Godwin clericus.	Agnes de Rudham and Geoffrey and Philip and Ralph her sons.
166	—	Helom Hoc.	*John son of Leuwine, and William son of Richard, Richard son of Elfreda, and Wic son of William.
167	—	*Nicholas Crawe and Avicia his wife.	Ralph de Torey.
168	—	William son of Asketel.	*Peter son of Ailric.
169	—	*Matilda q̅ fuit ux. Harlewin Kide.	Helias de Lond.
170	—	*William son of Christiana de Walsoken.	Helewisa dau. of Richard.

Description of Property.	Consideration, &c.
15 acres in Rokelund.	40ˢ sterling.
1½ perch of land in Cree.	10ˢ.
2 acres in Karston.	The regrant thereof at 4ᵈ yearly rent.
2 acres in Kareston.	The regrant thereof at 5ᵈ yearly rent.
4 acres in Wichchā.	12ˢ.
4 acres in Mouton. (†) 2⅓ˢ and half a rod of the said land, and of ¼ acre and 3 rods at Widehagedig, and 1 rod at Cademanesdale, and 1½ rod "apud pratū de Mout'," and 3 rods at Wieceric-heshove.	The regrant to Reginald of (†) at 6ᵈ every 20ˢ of scutage.
Half a messuage in Len, "et alia medietas remanet quieta ipi Raā ꞇ hēdibus suis in finem vij annoꝝ sequitm̄."	12ˢ.
2 shillings rent in Sipden.	The grant by Richard of the said rent to Roger de Reppes at 2ˢ yearly, Robert Buinard and his heirs to hold same of the said Roger at 2ˢ 6ᵈ yearly.
¼ of a knight's fee in Freton.	5 marks and 1 bizant.
4 acres in Brandon, to hold at the yearly service of 8ᵈ.	Half a mark.
15 acres in Rudham.	10 marks of silver.
5 acres in Letton.	The regrant thereof at 6ᵈ yearly.
40 acres in Hillington and a mill called Uvermilne, to hold to Ralph and his assigns, "præterquam viris religiosis," at the yearly rent of 9ˢ 8ᵈ.	100ˢ sterling.
Half an acre in Hikeford.	2ˢ sterling.
Her reasonable dower in Len, to hold at 6ᵈ yearly.	4 marks.
6 acres in Walsokene.	The regrant to Wm. of 2 acres thereof which lie to the north of her croft, at 13½ᵈ yearly.

No.	Date.	"Petens."	"Tenens."
171	10 Richard I.	*William Catelin (in body spelt Katelin.)	William son of William de Egesfeld (in body spelt Edesfield.)
172	—	William son of Hedmund.	*Alfred de (Tunstead?)
173	—	Goda daughter of Godwin Wisman.	*Walter Candel (or Caudel.)
174	—	Wimer son of William.	*Juliana and Emma daughters of Richard.
175	—	William and Osbert sons of Osketel.	*John son of Hugh.
176	—	*Guynilda de Morleic and Godiva de Depham.	Ralph del Hil.
177	—	*Segelin fil' William.	Ralph Clericus.
178	—	*Agnes vidua de Burnham and Walter her son.	Henry de Barsham.
179	—	William de Nes.	*Walter Cobbe.
180	—	*John son of Siric.	William son of Milo.
181	—	*Wido de Winterton.	William de Redham.

37

Description of Property.	Consideration, &c.
3 acres in Adelmerton (Aylmerton?)	. . .ᵍ
28 acres in Tunst̃.	The regrant of 3 parts of the whole of the said land, and 1 acre besides, at the yearly service of 16ˢ 7ᵈ, &c.
3 acres in Cree.	The grant to Walter of 1 acre in Alvodescroft, "et idem Walt̃ eidē godē i escambiū aliā acr̃ i Holegatehill."
20 acres in Srepham (Shropham?)	20ˢ of silver.
16 acres in Karboistorp. (†) Ita cū q̃d dedūt roābil escābiū p̃dco Johi t̃ hed suis p t̃eia pte p̃fat t̃re et sciedt ÷ q̃ dedūnt ei acr̃ t̃re in Scridehill in escabiū.	The regrant of ⅓ thereof at the yearly rent of 15ᵈ, except the capital messuage, which is to remain to William and Osbert (†)
13 acres in Depham. (†) 3 acres of the said ground, viz., 1 acre in Bubelescroft, 1 acre in Tuiceroft (?), ½ an acre at Buelond and ½ an acre at Ti⌐lwate (?) at 12ᵈ yearly rent.	10ˢ of silver for the dowers of the said Gunilda and Godiva, and also the regrant of (†)
12 acres in Horsted.	3ˢ sterling.
6 acres in Suderee.	2 bissants.
15 acres in Mantebi.	The regrant of half the said land to hold of the capital lord of the fee at 30ᵈ yearly.
8ᵈ rent issuing out of a messuage in Len, which the said William holds of Henry del Mareis.	10ˢ sterling.
15 acres in Vinterton and Sumerton. (†) 5 acres in Lillardescroft, 1 acre in Munekeswong, 1½ rod next the house of Goder . . . . towards the west, ½ acre next the mill of Ralph de Sumerton, 1½ rod at the head of the toft of Robert Pretoris, 3 rods at Mulehou, and 1 acre in Brom, to hold to William, the first named 5 acres	The regrant of (†)

No.	Date.	"Petens."	"Tenens."
182	10 Richard I.	*Gaufridus son of Warin.	Robert Briñiger.
183	—	*Laurence son of Token.	Alan son of William de Wigenhale.
184	—	*Hawis dau. of Margaret.	William de Briseworth and William son of Richard.
185	—	*William son of Gerard, and Richard his brother, and Staumerus son of Edwin.	Everard de Plumstede.
186	—	*Roger son of William, and Robert and Richard.	Robert le Gris.
187	—	*John son of Atketel.	Reinerus nephew of Leve.
188	—	*Gaufridus son of Wlmar.	William son of Claricia.
189	—	*Reginald and Runilda.	Robert and Edward de Blafeld (in body spelt Eduard and Ernald.)
190	—	*William son of Ralph de Len.	Adam son of Simon de Gernemue.
191	—	*Laurence son of Toke.	Robert son of Thomas and Heř his brother.
192	—	*Sefugell de Tunstall.	Eudo and Richard sons of Walter.

Description of Property.	Consideration, &c.
to revert after his death to Anne the dau. of Ralph de Sumerton and her heirs, to hold of the heirs of William at 12^d yearly rent.	
10 acres in Gillingham.	20^s sterling.
10 acres and 1 toft and 1 "salina" in Northlen.	30^s.
10 acres and 1 rood in Burnham.	3^s and the regrant to Hawis of (†)
(†) 2 acres and 1 rood, and 1 acre at Crokelundele and Beveresbure at 2^d yearly.	
9 acres in Plumstede.	The grant of 1½ acres in Aieg^{n}ve and ½ acre in Harescroft at 2^d yearly.
16 acres in Turton.	3 marks of silver.
7 acres in Lenn.	24^s sterling.
60 acres in Frenges.	The regrant of a tenement in Frenges, viz., 3 acres and 5 rods in the fields, and regrant of 16 acres, viz., 7 perches in Gateschiles, 5 rods in Lambecot, 3 acres in Estlangelond, 1 acre in Netherlaine, 3½ rods at the head of Lamecot, 1 acre at Gatlecrundel, 2½ acres in Spolinges, 3 rods at Newetongate, 3 rods at Rodulvesaker, 2 acres in Spotlinges, and 1½ acre in Redeland, to hold at 21^d yearly, and 4^d the 20^s of scutage.
20 acres in Blafeld.	The regrant of 3½ acres and 1 rod thereof at 7^d yearly.
1 "scouda" et loc̄ scoud ejusdem in Lennia apud fōr de Maresdi.	5^s sterling.
5 acres in Nordlen, and 5 acres of salt marsh in Wadhoge, and 1 "salina" and toft, &c.	1 mark of silver.
5½ acres in Tunstall.	10^s sterling.

No.	Date.	"Petens."	"Tenens."
193	10 Richard I.	*Odbert son of Godric.	Levinic, Gunilda, Beatrice, Elfleda, Langlina, and Guña, dau. of William de Thirine.
194	—	Hodiern⁹ fil' Siward.	*Ralph and William sons of Hedric.
195	—	Alan son of William.	*Godefrid son of Richard and Godefrid Scot.
196	—	*Morant son of Cruis and Botilda his wife and Rigware sister of Botilda.	Ralph de Langewade.
197	—	*Theobald son of Leffi.	Ralph de Curcun.
198	—	Hugh son of Avand.	*Matild Angot.
199	—	Galfridus Crawe of Strattune.	*Levare son of Turstan.
200	—	*Thurstan de Grimeston.	Gaufridus son of Wulvive.
201	—	*William de Nuieres.	William son of Roger.
202	—	Peter de Melton.	*Roger son of Gerold by Johanna his wife, and Ralph his brother.
203	—	William son of Oki and Godiva his wife.	*Gocelin Brais and William his brother.
204	—	*Henry son of Walter.	Thurbertus son of Roger ("Thurbñus" in body.)
205	—	Agnes daughter of Fulered.	*Roger Capellanus.
206	—	*Eustachius son of Walter.	Matilda Vidua and Radulphus her son.
207	—	*Wlviva de Syreford.	William de Cree.

Description of Property.	Consideration, &c.
12 acres in Thirne.	The grant of 1 rod, and half the acre called Helwine's acre, at 1ᵈ yearly rent.
6 acres, part of 9 acres in the fields of Sidesterne.	The release by Hodierna of remaining 3 acres.
9½ acres in Tilencia.	The grant of 2½ acres in the fields of Tilencia at Burwennes Neuheland.
60 acres and half the mill at Langwade.	28ˢ 8ᵈ sterling.
8 acres in Adelbure.	1 mark of silver.
3 acres in Wretton.	42ᵈ and the yearly rent of 9ᵈ.
3 acres in Stratun.	1 mark of silver.
4 acres in Grimeston.	8ˢ sterling.
30 acres in Saxlingham.	2 marks of silver.
¼ of a knight's fee in Saxlingham and Langham.	The regrant thereof (at the tenure of ¼ of a knight's fee and 2ˢ yearly) except Hobbescroft in the town of Saxlingham, and except all the arable land which Roger held in Langham, which are to remain to Peter.
2 acres in Wigehal. (*sic*—no abbreviation mark)	One bizant.
3 acres in Bunewell.	3ˢ.
8 acres in Ruieshal.	10ˢ.
4 acres in Woderoua.	The regrant of 1½ acre to Eustace, he doing his proportion of service to the capital Lord of the fee, and the payment to Eustace of 1 mark.
32 acres in Cree and Toftes.	For this and for the homage and service of William de Syreford, William de Cree grants

No.	Date.	"Petens."	"Tenens."
208	10 Richard I.	*Juliana and Matilda her sister.	William Russū.
209	—	*Walter Walese.	Nicholas son of Reginald.
210	—	Elfleda sister of Turstein.	*Baldewin son of Sedegos.
211	—	*Roger son of Abric and Hervald (Hernald ?) his son.	Aured Grei.
212	—	*Roger son of John.	William son of William.
213	—	*Milo son of Roger.	Agatha the wife of Wakelin de Besevilo
214	—	*Robert de Titleshall and Yvour his brother.	Herbert de Titleshal.

43

Description of Property.	Consideration, &c.
	to William de Syreford, the heir of the said Wlvive, 6 acres in Toftes, and also grants him 8 acres in the same place, to hold at 4ᵈ yearly, and 1ᵈ the 20ˢ of scutage.
1 carucate in Houton.	The regrant to Juliana and William her first-born son of 24 acres and 1 croft thereof, at 31½ᵈ yearly, and to Matilda and "Willielmo parvo filio suo" of 19½ acres in the fields of Houton, and 1 curtilage next the "marā" of Houton, at 2ˢ yearly.
4 acres, being part of 8 acres in Herdhwic.	The quit claim of the other 4 acres, viz., 1 acre lying between the house of Richard Baret and the house of Osegot, 1½ acre "juxta antiquam viam," and 1½ acre in Bruneshage to hold to Walter, at 8ᵈ yearly.
Half of 3 acres in Limpenhōg.	3ˢ and the quit claim of the other half.
7 acres in Senctesham.	20ˢ sterling "p̄ dotüs aurēd p̄diē Rogo et H⁹vald p̄diē."
5 acres in Wauton.	The regrant of half thereof, at 3ᵈ yearly rent.
6 acres in Hadestune.	The regrant of 2½ acres thereof in Haddestune, viz., in Riccroft, at 4ᵈ yearly, and 1ᵈ the 20ˢ of scutage.
30 acres in Titleshal and Gremeston.	The payment to Robert of 2 marks, and the grants to Yvour of 6 acres in Gremeston, viz., Ridecroft

No.	Date.	"Petens."	"Tenens."
215	10 Richard I.	Radulphus son of Ribald.	*Robert Bedell.
216	—	Rand[ulphus] son of Robert.	*Radulphus son of Roger.
217	—	*Herveus son of Juliana.	Agnes de Francsham.
218	—	*Robert de Riflai.	Matilda, Prioress of the Church of St. Mary de Karhoge, Gosebert de Senteler, Umfry de Erlham, and Alicia Peverel (by Adam, presbiter de Lakenham, in the place of the Prioress, and Gilbert son of Vivien in the place of Senteler.)
219	—	*Radulphus Avenant.	Thomas de Burgo.
220	—	*Thiedā de Westwen, and Alan, Godwin, Osbert, and Gaufridus, his sons.	William son of Leowin Crisp.
221	—	*Robert de Pinkenei.	William his brother.

Description of Property.	Consideration, &c.
4 acres in Rūhau. (Runhall ?)	and Pacewineslund, and 1 acre at Norhhill, at 8ᵈ yearly. The regrant for life of 1 acre 1 rod in a croft, ½ an acre in Bunescroft, and 1 rod upon the Hill.
8 acres in Parvo Ribure [except 1½ acre in Kilnecroft, instead of which Ralph gives Randle 2 acres in Milliecroft and Hundemilhe.	10ˢ sterling and the yearly rent of 2ˢ.
1 carucate of land in Franesham.	1 mark of silver, and the regrant to Hervey at 3ᵈ yearly of (†)
(†) 20 acres in Franesham, viz., 5½ acres "ad Longam Terram," 4 acres "ad Curtam Terram," 3 acres "ad portam ecclesie de Franesham," 3 acres in Tofto Ailrich, 3 acres in Tofto Juliane, and ½ acre "de terra Brictmari."	
7ˢ rent in Meleť (Melton), to hold to Matilda and her successors by the will and assent of the other parties.	20ˢ sterling (paid by the Prioress.)
30 acres in Tudenham.	1 mark.
9 acres in Westwinic and Sech (Setchy).	7ˢ sterling.
Half a knight's fee in Brunstorp.	The regrant to Robert, at the service of ¼ of a knight's fee, of half the said land, except 13 acres of marsh, which the said William gave to the Canons of the Church of St. Mary of Rudham (and instead of which 13 acres, William gave

No.	Date.	"Petens."	"Tenens."
222	10 Richard I.	*Philip son of Robert.	Daniel de M')lay parson of the Church of Flich.
223	—	Roger son of Robert de Saixlingham.	*John son of Nicholas de Dallinge.
224	—	*Benedict and Ida his wife.	Andrew de Tirinton and Muriel his wife, and Robert son of Harlewin and Agnes his wife, and Peter son of Godwin.
225	—	*Philip de Burnham and Fracr (?) and Roger his brothers.	Martin de Warkles.
226	—	*Gilbert de Berton.	William de Hengham.
227	—	*Amindus son of Wulvive.	Agnes, who was the wife of Bernard Brun, and William her son.

Description of Property.	Consideration, &c.
	Robert other 3 acres, viz., 1½ acre in Brūstorp and 1½ acre in Kirkedele towards the east), saving (as to the whole) the dower of Alice their mother in Bruneston (*sic*). If Robert should die without heirs by his wife, the land granted to him to revert to William, and after the death of Alice their mother half her dower to revert to each of William and Robert.
8 acres in Flich[am] and Satton, which Philip acknowledges to be free alms to the said Church by the gift of his father Robert.	
30 acres in Oueltun.	The regrant thereof to John for life, at the rent of 22^s, 2^s whereof go to Roger, and 20^s to the capital Lord of the fee.
54 acres in Wauton.	40^s and the yearly rent of 5^s and 3^d every 20^s of scutage.
1 carucate in Bunħtorp.	
(†) Half the said land (except the advowson of the Church of St. Peter of Burnhtorp and except the capital messuage) to hold of Martin at 15^s rent. Instead of the capital messuage Martin grants to Stephen a croft and a messuage which were of Turke in the same town.	The grant to Stephen son of Bartholomew, decanus de Wallingham, and his heirs in marriage with Johanna, sister of the said Philip, &c., of (†)
60 acres in Welle and in [Hengham].	The release of Gilbert from 3^s, which he pays to William on land he holds at Berton—Gilbert however paying William 2^s on the 20^s of scutage.
Half an acre in Martham.	4^s sterling (paid by Agnes.)

No.	Date.	"Petens."	"Tenens."
228	10 Richard I.	*Auxstin de Tunsted and Adam his brother.	Walter Draf and Estrilda his wife and Walter son of Estrilda.
229	—	*Bertram capellanus and Guido and Jocelin his brothers.	Albert Faber and John his brother.
230	—	*Radulphus son of Peter.	William de Fossa?.
231	—	William and Hawis his wife, and Alice her sister.	*Benedict son of Thurkild.
232	—	*William le Cat.	Richard and Godefrey.
233	—	*Robert Noc.	Galfridus and Alan fil' Ade.
234	—	*Matilda daughter of Levive.	Emelina de Billokebi.
235	—	*Richard son of Dove.	Philip de Snariges.
236	—	*Peter son of Galfridus de Holkam.	Vincentius, clericus de Surligham.

Description of Property.	Consideration, &c.
12 acres in Suaneton.	½ a mark of silver.
6 acres in Waketun.	The regrant of (†) Bertram, Guido, and Jocelin in return pay Albert and John 1 mark of silver, and grant to them (††)
(†) Half the said land (which Herbert, capellanus, held of Sibilla de Castre) at 3¼ᵈ yearly.	
(††) Half that land (which they held in Waketun of Emma and Galiena of the fee of the said Sibilla) at 1ᵈ yearly.	
21 acres in Atleburg and Elingham.	The yearly rent of 18ᵈ and one pound of cummin, and the quit claim by William of his right in (†)
(†) Half a virgate of land *in Warrewicsyre in villa de Morton*.	
8 acres (?) in Marlingeford.	The yearly rent of 3ᵈ and the regrant of (†)
(†) The capital messuage and 1 acre 1 rod in Estmedewe, and 1 rod of arable land sub cur (tilagium) of William and Hawis.	
14 acres in Hormesbi.	The regrant of (†)
(†) 5 acres thereof, viz., 1 acre in the croft which was of Robert le Butilier, 1 acre in Holmo, 1 acre in Killingewro, ½ an acre in Hes, ½ an acre juxta Wintertunegate, ½ an acre in Hoddehoge, and ½ an acre in Toftes, to hold of the Prior of Norwich at 10¼ᵈ yearly (William paying half a mark.)	
16 acres in Kimberllee.	Half a mark.
1½ acre in Clipesbi.	The grant of ½ an acre in Billokebi "apud boscum Ricardi de Clipesbi," at 7ᵈ yearly rent.
16 acres in Toftes.	The regrant of 6 acres thereof, at the yearly service of 12ᵈ and 1ᵈ the 20ˢ of scutage.
42 acres in Surligham.	6 marks to Peter and half a mark to his wife (no name given), and the rent of 4ˢ and 1ᵈ the 20ˢ of scutage. Conveyance "viris religiosis" barred, as in No. 167.

No.	Date.	"Petens."	"Tenens."
237	10 Richard I.	*Radulfus capellanus.	William Brito.
238	—	*William son of Ave.	Ralph de Scois.
239	—	*Wlmar son of Hugh.	Reginald de Rya.
240	—	*Clement son of Richard.	Robert son of Richard.
241	—	*Gocelin son of Leffi.	Roger Puting.
242	—	*Bartholomew de Runhal, Roger de Reppes, and Gilbert de Runhal. [Eustachius, and Mabilia the wife of Roger de Reppes, are also mentioned in the body of the fine as grantors.]	William, Prior of the Church of St. Mary and All Saints of West Acre.
243	—	*Wlmar son of Hugh.	Lefeini who was the wife of Hedric.
244	—	*Godwin Parmtar.	Robert son of Aselac.
245	—	*Hervicius son of Peter.	Leva daughter of Geoffrey.
246	—	*Ailmer son of Walter Freland.	John Lōgū.
247	—	*William Battaile and William de Huntingefeld and Ysabella his wife.	William Brito.

Description of Property.	Consideration, &c.
20 acres in Sweingtune, which Ralph, with the consent of William Brito, grants to William Batalie (sic).	The grant by William Batvill (sic) to Ralph of (†)
(†) A messuage "juxta alneṯ ipsius Willielmi Bataill (sic) in Sweingtun," to hold for Ralph's life, at 1^d yearly.	
50 acres in Rudham.	10^s, 3 "minas ordei," and the regrant of (†)
(†) 4 acres and 3 rods thereof, viz., 2 acres 1 rood juxta Herpelegate, ½ an acre in Silescroft, ½ an acre juxta viam de Ilneford (?), 3 rod juxta viam de Massingham, and ½ an acre in Bolohogedel; to hold of Ralph at 3^d yearly.	
Half a messuage in Lenn.	2^s sterling.
25 acres in Hindolvestun.	40^s sterling.
16 acres in Hekingham.	20^s sterling and the regrant of 2 acres thereof, to hold of the capital lord of the fee at 8^d yearly.
The advowson of the Church of Runhal.	A gold ring and the grant to Bartholomew, &c., "pticipes fieri omĩum bonoʒ q̃ fiũnt i p̃dca ecclia de Westacĩ."
Half a messuage in Linn.	2^s sterling.
2 acres in Sydestne.	The regrant of 1 acre thereof which lies at the west end of the toft of Bonde, at 1^d yearly.
12 acres in Pikenham.	1 mark of silver.
3 acres in Wiclewde.	Half a mark.
60 acres in Sueingeton, Aldreford, Feletorp, Attlebrige, Mortun, Wichingeham, Weston, and Taverham, and the advowsons of the churches of Sweiningeton, Aldreford, and Felthorp, to hold of William Bataill of William de Huntingfield and Isabella his wife.	[The service of] ⅛ of a knight's fee and 40^s yearly. William Bataill pays William de Huntingefield 10 marks of silver and Isabel 2 marks, and also grants to Wil-

No.	Date.	"Petens."	"Tenens."
248	10 Richard I.	*Wlvivia sister of Edric.	Adam the son of Robert and Emma his wife.
249	—	Simon son of Randulph.	*Roger son of Hane (?)
250	—	John son of Turstan.	*Alan his brother.
251	—	*Richard son of Julian.	Matilda daughter of Gocelin.
252	—	Yvo son of Richard.	*Earl Roger and Countess Gundreda, by Roger de Braham, seneschal of the Earl, and Geoffrey de Brokes, seneschal of the Countess.
253	—	Simon son of Rikolf.	*Walter son of Wimunde.
254	—	*Hamo son of William.	Walter de Dunham.
255	—	*Gilbert son of Henry.	William de Uphale.
256	—	*William Buffum (Buffiun?)	Deodonatus Kide.
257	—	Roger de B\^a(ndon?)	*Bartholomew de Edisfield and Matilda his wife.
258	—	*Fulcher Brito.	Ralph de Wesenham.
259	—	*Reiner son of Osbert and Ailea his wife, and Roger Quarter and Engeleda his wife.	William son of Wlnad, Godiva vidua, and Emma vidua.
260	—	*Beatrix daughter of William.	Richard de Bretham.
261	—	*Radulf son of Turstan.	Jocelin Feutrarius.
262	—	*William de Nordwolde.	John son of Lambert and Stephen his brother.

Description of Property.	Consideration, &c.
	liam Brito at 20ˢ yearly for the latter's life [vide No. 237.]
4 acres in Dallinge.	The regrant to Wlviva of
(†) ½ an acre at Crundeland, 1 rod at Witmererod, and 1 rod at Ringenuse (?) at 4ᵈ yearly.	(†)
1¼ acre in . . . . . sted.	The regrant thereof to Roger to hold of the capital lord of the fee, at 3ᵈ yearly.
Half of 24 acres and 1 toft in Wigēhaude to hold of the capital Lord of the fee, at 18ᵈ yearly. The other half to remain to Alan on similar service. If John should die without issue by his wife his moiety to revert to Alan.	None.
12 acres in Renham.	1 mark of silver.
1 carucate in Loppham.	The regrant to Yvo of half the land to hold at 5ˢ yearly (mentions Godwin prepositus of Lopham.)
A messuage in Lenn.	3½ marks of silver.
7½ acres in Dunham.	6ᵈ of silver.
7 acres in Assebi.	1 mark of silver.
A messuage in Len.	3½ marks of silver.
The advowson of half the church of All Saints of Bᵃndon.	10ˢ sterling.
8 acres in Weseham, to hold of Walter de Hoo at service of 12ᵈ yearly, and at yearly rent to Fulcher of a pound of cummin.	20ˢ.
18 acres in Lenn.	8ˢ.
30 acres in Bretham.	Half a mark of silver and the regrant to hold of Richard and his heirs for ever.
A messuage in Len.	43ˢ.
40 acres and a messuage in Wesenham.	2 marks of silver.

No.	Date.	"Petens."	"Tenens."
263	10 Richard I.	*Henry son of Lambert.	John son of Godiva.
264	—	*Hugh son of Wlveve.	Richard son of Stanild.
265	—	Peter son of Walter, and Godiva daughter of Thoke.	*Godwin son of Gutfrith.
266	—	*Richard son of Ysaac.	Robert de Cree.
267	—	*Alured son of Walter.	Ralph Carpentarius and Basilia his wife.
268	—	*Richard Turbern and Maria his wife.	Agatha de Haddestun.
269	—	*Rignare sister of Hervey de Dudewic.	Hermer de Banton and Gilbert his son.
270	—	Safrei son of William.	*Ranulph son of Richard.
271	—	*Hugh and Roger sons of Toch.	Geoffrey Braid.
272	—	*Walter son of Ketel.	Richard de Refham.
273	—	William son of Edmund.	*Alfred de Dustale.
274	—	*Richard son of William.	Ralph son of Richard and Thure his mother.
275	—	*Godwin son of Swetman.	Gomel son of Hereward.
276	—	*Ralph son of Thedric.	Richard son of Thedric.
277	—	*Wlvav.	Hamo de Dockinges.

Description of Property.	Consideration, &c.
18 acres in Cree.	2 marks of silver.
7½ acres in Horstede.	2 marks of silver.
12 acres in Westweniz.	2 marks of silver.
30 acres in Dunstun.	The grant thereof to Hubert de Broo at the service of one-16th of a knight's fee, the grant to Richard of 13 acres of land, to hold at the service of 3^d and 1^d for every 20^s of scutage, and 2 marks of silver.
7 acres in Coleton.	The grant to Alured of 2 acres . . . . at Wellegate . . . . Leavines . . . Gailecroft . . . . . . Holandegat . . . . and Bahardeshowe, to hold at 3 oboli yearly.
One-fifth of a knight's fee in Haddestun.	4 marks of silver.
4 acres in Dudewic.	The regrant of 4 acres in . . . . Hevedemere . . . . Stanhal . . . Smalethornes . . . . and Bradegate, and one mark.
5½ acres in Branton.	Half a mark.
2 acres in Sparham.	3^s of silver.
1 rod in Kyneholm.	4^s sterling and yearly sum of 1^d.
28 acres in Dūstale.	2 marks of silver.
28 acres in Rudham.	Half a mark of silver and the regrant of an acre of the said land in Faremaneswag, to hold at 2^d yearly.
8 acres in Wychal and Helsingeton.	2 marks of silver and half of 2 acres in the fields of Tilencie.
6 acres in Weston.	24^s sterling.
30 acres in Sudmere.	The regrant of half thereof, except his enclosed mes-

No.	Date.	"Petens."	"Tenens."
278	10 Richard I.	*Robert Berlupeinne.	Adam de Houeton.
279	—	*Richard son of William and Richilda his wife.	Herbert son of William.
280	—	*Ralph son of Roger.	John his brother.
281	—	*Geoffrey Toke.	Espeland de Gernemuť.
282	—	Roger de Ho.	*Robert de Morlay and Roger de Gessinge.
283	—	Robert de Mortuomari.	*Henry T')nccurt.
284	—	*Henry de Marisco.	*Laurence capellanus.
285	—	*Simon son of Roger de Cherevile.	Robert son of Walter de Cherevill.

Description of Property.	Consideration, &c.
	suage, to hold of Hamo at 2^d yearly, for which regrant Wivay pays 6 marks.
24 acres in Tunsted.	The release to Robert of 2^d out of 30^d yearly rent he owed Adam for 30 acres of land.
30 acres in Dunstan. (†) 3 rods at the head of the croft of Everard Bisop, 2 parts of an acre in Hungerdale, 2 parts of an acre in Lambig^{a}ve, 2 parts of ½ an acre at the head of the croft of Herbert in the acre of Bruni in Lund, ½ an acre in Northfurlang, and ½ an acre in Westgaletonēd.	The grant in exchange of 4 acres of said land and 18^d, viz. (†) To hold of Herbert at 7^d yearly.
13 acres in Parva Rigsted.	The regrant of half thereof to hold of the capital lord at 4^d yearly, so that Ralph and his heirs should hold 7 acres of it for their mother's life.
15 acres in Hales.	2 marks of silver.
Common of pasture in Brisingeham, Ridinge, and Selfhangre.	1 bisant.
"Una mara q̃ vocat^r Miclem̃e que ÷ sub curia p̃dci Rob ⁊ 1 magn̄ fossāt qd̄ ÷ ex^a p̃dcam marā ⁊ 1 pecata t̃re de lōgo ⁊ lōgū p̃dci fossati ⁊ fossāt p̃dēm ⁊ c^{o}ftū p̃dci Henric̄ ⁊ Coligton."	The grant in exchange of 11 pieces of meadow "in latitudine que jacet juxta curiā p̃dci Henr̄ ⁊ decipūt ad c^{o}ftū p̃dci Henrii ⁊ t̃minat ad cursū cujusdā aque."
A messuage in Lenn.	20^s sterling by the consent of Gerard, Prior of Norwich, "ad quem (*sic*) pertinet d̃)mū fundi."
9 acres in Tilneie.	2 marks of silver and also 4^d out of 2^s service for a messuage in Tillencie, between the land of Turvis de Wigenhale and the land of Rod son of Godwin.

58

No.	Date.	"Petens."	"Tenens."
286	10 Richard I.	Michael Chevere (or Chenere.)	*William de Huntingfend and Isabel his wife.
287	—	*Walter son of Aildrick.	Nicholas son of Algar.
288	—	Adam son of Robert.	*John son of William.
289	—	Wimar de Hocham.	*Ralph Magnū.
290	—	*William and Lewana his wife.	Adam Le Yvvelhume.
291	—	*Peter son of Botilda.	Elias son of Elias.
292	—	*Ede daughter of Walter.	Simon Mager.
293	—	*Gregory son of Peter de Suapham.	William, Eustace, and Godfrey, his brothers.
294	—	*Christiana daughter of Peter de Billokebi.	Nicholas de Haledis.
295	—	*Roger Talebot and Katherine his wife.	Agatha daughter of Wilde Haddestune.
296	—	Alexander son of Richard.	*Richard Parmentarius and Muriel his wife.
1	1 John.	*Lecia daughter of Ralph Camerarius by John her son.	Philip de Bretheham.
2	—	*Gilbert de Tudeham.	Simon de Huntedun.
3	—	Ralph de Benham.	*Gaufridus son of Wimund.
4	—	*Herveus son of William.	Ralph son of (Geoffrey?)
5	—	Peter de Watligton.	*Ernald de Il')laue.

Description of Property.	Consideration, &c.
2 carucates of land in Wellingham, "uñ duellū concussū fuit inter eos ī p̄fata cūr."	The regrant for ever at the service of half a knight's fee, for which William paid 30 marks of silver.
4 acres 4 rods in Winterton.	The regrant at 30^d yearly.
40 acres in Tibeham to hold of John at 4^d yearly, "And Roger, the elder brother of the said Adam, comes into Court and quits claim of the said land to the said Adam for one bisant and Adam gives to John 16^s sterling."	
1 carucate in Quideham.	20^s sterling and an annuity to Ralph of 12^d.
2 acres in Flokestorp.	6^s sterling.
40 acres in Dallinge.	The regrant of part of the said land, viz., in Blacheho .... Brādal .... Lāghāgate ... Lāhābush and Colecroft at 16^d yearly.
..... in Kinesthorp.	A mark of silver.
35 acres in Suvaphā.	The regrant of 7½ acres at 12^d in ... Wodegate ... Packelowe and Fortleg.
One-sixth of 60 acres in Billokebi.	30^s sterling
One-fifth of a knight's fee in Haddestune.	1 mark of silver.
2½ virgates and 3 bovates of land in Kittona.	12 marks of silver "in denariis."
40 acres in Geiton.	4 marks of silver.
1 carucate of land in Thornham.	6 marks of silver.
17 acres in Wicton.	The regrant thereof to Geoffrey at 3^s and 1^d, Geoffrey also pays 16^s sterling.
40 acres in Barham.	2½ marks of silver.
A messuage and 10^s rent in Lowingeh.	10 marks of silver.

No.	Date.	"Petens."	"Tenens."
6	1 John.	*Robert son of Swein.	The Abbot of Ramsey by Reiner the monk.
7	—	*John de Fridh.	William son of Turgis.
8	—	Ralph de Tasseburc.	*Matthew son of Richard.
9	—	Alan de Beauteis.	*Simon son of John.
10	—	*William de Bello Monte and Muriel his wife, by William Houel.	Gilbert de Langetot.
11	—	*Godfrey de Lisewis.	Gilbert Pauper (son of Godfrey Pauper.)
12	—	Ralph de Benham.	*Ralph son of Goldwin.
13	—	*Robert de Bosco and Eva his wife.	Robert de Sandecroft.

Description of Property.	Consideration, &c.
64 pieces ("peat") of turbary in the marsh of Stowe.	A messuage in the town of St. Ives (subject as herein mentioned) and a mark of silver.
4½ acres in Wigenhale.	4 acres (less one rood) in Wigenhale, viz., 2¼ acres in the field which is called Severode, and 1 acre 1 rood in the field which is called Gildegore, at 6^d yearly.
12 acres and a messuage in Tasseburc.	17^s 0½^d yearly rent and 40^s sterling.
A messuage in Lenn.	The regrant of the said messuage to hold of Adam son of Simon de Gernemue at 2^s yearly, which Adam is to pay to Alan 12^d yearly: Simon pays to Alan 5 marks of silver.
2⅓ knights' fees in Saxlingeham, Binetre, Ikeburc, and Wichingham.	A hawk and the service of 2⅙ knights' fees.
The services, &c., which belonged to the said Godfrey, for a tenement which Gilbert held of him in Reinham, viz., of all the land which Ralph Largus held in Reinham, and of 2 pieces of land in Suthmorfurlang and of Sortchardlond, and of a piece of land at Estmor, and of the meadow which is of the fee of the said Godfrey between Prestebrige and the pool of Suthreinham, and of 6 pieces of turbary at Brātesfurlang, and of the croft which Safred held, and half an acre at the head of the said croft.	To hold at the service named in a charter from Godfrey to Gilbert (as therein set out at length.)
12 acres in Wigton.	10^s 8^d and the yearly rent of 26^d.
2 carucates in Elmcham and Humesfeld, claimed as dower of Eva from the gift of Barthol. de Sandcroft late her husband.	30 acres in Humesfeld, viz., 21 acres 1 rood in Dimigedal and 1½ acre and 1 rood in Alwineshill, to hold for the life of Eva at 23½^d yearly rent.

Date.	"Petens."	"Tenens."
John.	Henry de Fleg.	*Abbraam and Matilda his wife.
—	*Robert son of Angod.	Ralph son of Angod.
—	*William, Abbot of Becco, and the convent of the same place, by Hugh the monk.	Wimer de Hooham.
—	*Ysmaina daughter of Warin Hostiarius.	Alice de Gernemue and Ada her daughter.
—	Richard (torn).	*Simon son of Peter de Stowe.

Description of Property.	Consideration, &c.
3 messuages in Gernemue.	The grant to Abraam and Matilda of "domū lapideā integ° cū tota rēgatu ubi sita ÷ domus illa a chimino usq̄ ī aq^{a}m" at 7^s 8^d yearly.
¼ of a carucate of land in Cangham.	The regrant of 6 acres thereof, viz., 3 acres "ad maram" and 3 acres "sub Scarbotewell," at 30^d yearly.
"De una falda in Wrotthā injuste levata ut p̃dcus abbas dix :" (240 sheep.)	60^s sterling.
2 messuages in Lenn, of which one is in the street of St. James and the other in Tuesday Market Place ("in foro martis") and contained in length 100 feet, and in breadth 40 feet.	5½ marks and the yearly rent of 3^s.
A messuage in Welle.	The regrant of the eastern half thereof with its appurtenances, namely, of the 30 acres lying between "La Drave" and Hermitesheie, the half lying towards the south, and of 20 other acres lying between La Drave and Hermiteshie, the half lying toward the south, and in Wadinges 3 acres and 1 rood, and half the toft which Swetman held towards the south, and half the meadow at Ratlesbech toward the north, and all the meadow which Stannard held in (Radelād?) and of certain shares of rights of fishing on certain nights at certain places, (as therein set out at length).

No.	Date.	"Petens."	"Tenens."
19	1 John.	William de Muleton and Alice his wife	*Agatha de Haddeston.
20	—	*Hugh de Bernard.	Richard son of Walter.
21	—	*Stephen son of Reginald.	Peter Bardulf.
22	—	*William de Warenn.	Ralph de Curcun.
23	—	*Warin, Simon, and Robert de Colebi, by William de Pirho.	William de Burc and Simon de Crakeford.
24	—	Thomas Prior of Binham.	*Ralph de Dallinges.
25	—	*Adam decanus of Burneham.	Stephen de Walsingham.
26	—	Ralph son of David and Inca his mother.	*Aubertus son of Bund.
27	—	*Magister Reginald de Lenn and William son of Ralph.	Alice de Gernemue and Adam her son.
28	—	*Helewisa who was the wife of Wm. de Houton.	Richard son of Galfridus.
29	—	*Magister Reginald de Len.	William son of Ralph.

Description of Property.	Consideration, &c.
One-fifth of a knight's fee in Haddestun, of which Agatha grants 3 acres lying under the wood of Fulco Bainald towards the west, and 3 acres in Bunegerescroft, and 2 acres next the mere, to William and Alice, at the service of one-40th part of a knight's fee.	Agatha pays 40^s sterling, and William and Alice quit their claim on the remainder of the one-fifth fee.
11 acres of land, and 6 acres of wood, and 2½ acres of meadow, and 2 acres of pasture in Taculnestun, and 9 acres of land and ½ an acre of wood in Fornesset.	20^s sterling and 3 acres in Tacolneston to hold at 4^d yearly.
2 carucates in Spichesworth.	15 marks of silver.
The advowson of the church of Jackesham.	A hawk (ostorius).
Half the advowson of the church of Coleby.	The other half to remain to Warin, Simon, and Robert.
40 acres in Parva Ribure.	The regrant thereof at 6^s yearly.
40 acres and a messuage in Burnehamtorp which were of Harvey Sacerdos.	5 marks of silver and the regrant of the premises to Adam for his life at 3^d yearly.
Half a messuage in Lenne.	The regrant thereof at 6^d yearly, for which Aubert pays 4 marks.
A salt pit, &c., in Lenn.	40^s sterling and the yearly rent of 12^d and 3 "cumbar sal."
18 acres in Houhton claimed as dower.	40^s sterling.
Half a messuage and of a rent of 12^s, and half of 8½ stalls (seldarum), and half of a salt pit and a half, and half of 6 acres and 3 rods of land in Len and West Weniz.	3½ marks of silver and 2 marks of rent in Len, viz., Mag^r Wm. de Len 12^d, Laurence capellanus 12^d, Jocelin de Walepol 3^s, Stephen de Walsingham 7^s 6^d, William son of Richard 8^d, Henry his brother 8^d, Richard Noth 6^d, Ralph Kelloc 8^d, Wm. son of Milo 8^d, Richard de Bretham 12^d, Wm. son of Simon 18^d,

F

No.	Date.	"Petens."	"Tenens."
30	1 John.	*Ralph de Lenham.	Walter de Ainels (?)
31	2 John.	Roger de Kerdeston.	*Milo de Noiers.
32	—	*William de Kaiou.	The Prior of Binham.
33	—	*William de Raimes.	John de Reinestorp.
34	—	*Thomas son of Walter.	William, Parson of Meaudon (*sic*).
35	—	*Alice de Kailly by Peter de Bathe.	John de Cailly.
36	—	*Ralph Mercator.	Gerberg de Gernemue.
37	—	*Godwin Parmentar.	Humphry son of Siward.
38	—	*John Marescall and Alina his wife, and Gaufrid Cestr and Ysabel his wife.	Roger de Kerdeston.
39	—	Robert de Erpingeham.	Peter de Alto Bosco.

Description of Property.	Consideration, &c.
	Robert de Cibctei 12^d, Gaufrid de Sechford 16^d, Leman de Wlwreton 12^d, Galfrid de Sangham 6^d, William Kide 12^d, Osbert Kirmetre 16^d, Richard son of Swenild 6^d, and Isaac son of Jurnet 22^d, to hold all these for ever at the yearly service of 1 lb. of cummin. Cross remainders in case of death of either William or Reginald without heirs.
Half the manor of Reddenhal.	12 marks of silver and the yearly service of one-and-a-half knight's fee.
A third of certain common of pasture in Swanton.	A black horse of the 3rd year, and one of the 6th year.
"De Secta et consuetudinibus quas idem Willelmus dixit pertinere ad Hundredum suum de Wicton."	William and his heirs to be quit of toll in the market of Binham.
Half a knight's fee in Reinestorp.	100^s sterling.
2 carucates of land in Meauton.	3 marks of silver.
A carucate of land in Hildeburchworth.	None.
A messuage in Gernemue, which William Mercator held.	40^s sterling.
6 acres in Sidesterne.	The regrant of 3 acres to the east thereof at 3^d yearly.
Half a knight's fee in Newton.	100 marks of silver and the service of half a knight's fee.
Advowson of Erpingham. Half thereof to remain to Robert and half to Peter.	Peter grants to Robert 3 acres in Erpingham, lying at Holegatesende "de feud Cordebof versus austř monastii de Erpingeham" at a lb. of pepper yearly.

No.	Date.	"Petens."	"Tenens."
40	2 John.	*Richard son of Robert.	The Prior of Binham.
41	—	*Peter de Beches and Beatrix his wife.	John de Kailli.
42	—	*Brian son of Ralph.	Milo de Hastings.
43	—	*Robert son of Pagan.	Simon his brother.
44	—	*Clement de Dockinges.	William Luvel.
45	—	Alan de Mundeham.	*William de Sparham.
46	—	*William de Eboraco and Matilda his wife.	William son of Anketill and Thieda his wife, and William Wade and Alveva his wife.
47	3 John.	Robert de Vaus.	*Robert son of Wlfach.
48	—	*Robert Crowe.	Ganfridus Crawe his eldest son.

Description of Property.	Consideration, &c.
...... in Welles. (†) 6 acres in Magna Walsingham which Bartholomew son of Warin held, and 5 acres which Hago held, and 1 croft which the said Richard held in Welles, to hold at 1 lb. of pepper yearly.	The grant in exchange of (†)
2 carucates of land in Denever.	The grant to Beatrix as dower for her life of (†)
(†) "Tota villa de Crenewiz cum pertinentibus."	
A knight's fee in Quideham.	20 marks of silver.
"Et si p̄dcus Brianus potit recupare servic̄ p̄dci feod unius militis v̄sus Willm̄ de Munchanesi p̄dictus Milo ꝯcessit qd̄ hoc bn̄ stet."	
Robert's share of the land which was of Pagan their father in Hakeford, Coleby, and Felmingham.	6 marks of silver and all Simon's land held in fee in Felmingham [7½ acres ?] at 6ᵈ yearly.
24 acres in Sume.	The grant of (†)
(†) 2 acres between ....gate and Brancestregate which lay next the garden of Ralph Rikan, and 7 acres in Lukedonhel towards the east, and 1 acre in a croft, viz., towards the east, whereon to build a messuage, in the town of Doking, to hold at 10ᵈ yearly.	
A carucate in Riburg (Ralph de Dalling is mentioned.)	The regrant thereof at 6ᵈ yearly, for which William pays 40ᵈ sterling.
Matilda's share of the free tenement which was of her grandfather Reiner Salmar.	.... marks of silver, the messuage which the said Reiner gave in marriage with Estilda his daughter the mother of the said Matilda, and one-third of the capital messuage of Reiner in Lenn.
2 carucates in	The service of one-fourth of a knight's fee.
A carucate in Stratton to hold to him and his assigns, "præterquam viris religiosis," and 7 acres in Stratton, viz., 3 acres in Offrichestoft and 4 acres at the gate or door of Elen (?) Cupere.	(Natural love and affection ?)

No.	Date.	"Petens."	"Tenens."
49	3 John.	*Henry de Marisco.	Henry Pincerna and Juliana his sister and Henry her son.
50	—	*Simon Burell.	Tebb de Aldeburg and William his son.
51	—	Robert de Sudale by Simon son of Simon.	*Ralph son of Turlac.
52	—	*Hermar de Limesie.	Gilbert Abbot of Langeleḡ.
53	—	*Maria daughter of William de Hadescou.	...... her sister.
54	—	*Matilda daughter of William.	William son of Jocelin.
55	—	William Bataill (?)	*Roger Muloisell.
56	4 John.	*Hawisa Pictav̄ (iensis ?)	William de Estiñ.
57	—	*Costinus son of William.	Safred de Rungeton.
58	—	Hubert son of Gregory.	*Geoffrey Ridell.
59	—	*Jocelin de Lewd ...	Godfrey Colebec.
60	—	Thomas son of Geoffrey de Lineford.	*Richard de Risinge.
61	—	*Thomas de Ingaldestorp and Sibilla his wife.	Hermor de Bekeswell.

Description of Property.	Consideration, &c.
40 acres in Hemested and Bodeham, to hold at 4ˢ yearly (except as therein mentioned.)	The remission of (†)
(†) A carucate of land in Hemsted and Bodeham which the said Henry Pincerna claimed against the said Henry de Marisco.	Henry Pincerna also pays 2 marks of silver.
40 acres in Aldeburg.	1 mark of silver.
21 acres in Plumsted, B°ingham, and Wlterton.	20ˢ sterling.
A carucate in Langeleḡ.	40 marks of silver.
One-fourth of the lands and tenements which were formerly of their father in Bunewell, Carleton Rode, and Tibenham (?)	24 marks of silver.
The reasonable dower of the said Matilda, formerly the wife of Ralph, in Morleḡ.	22ˢ sterling.
6 acres in	The regrant thereof to Roger at 6ᵈ yearly, for which regrant Roger quits claim to William his right in certain premises abutting on the garden of Robert Tucke, &c.
Land which was of Geoffrey de Estim̄ in Thorp.	The regrant of 12 acres 3 roods thereof which lie next Erlesmilne, and the house which was of Geoffrey Pictav̄, and 1½ acre, &c., &c., abutting on the messuage of William Waleys, &c. .... in Wildeker, ... next Haghenildford, &c.
2 acres in Siceche.	1 mark of silver.
30 acres in Ykeburg.	20ˢ sterling.
A messuage and 6 acres in Hecham.	30ˢ sterling.
Half a carucate of land in Lineford to hold at half a mark yearly.	3 marks.
The reasonable dower of the said Sibilla, formerly the wife of Peter de Bekeswell, in Bekeswell, Dunham, Fordham, Crempleshain, Stradshete, Finchele, Helingeia, Westacre, ...echā, Rokesham, Tilneia, Terington, Walsocne, Wiggehal, Marham,	23ˢ a year rent in Marham to Sibilla for her life.

No.	Date.	" Petens."	"Tenens."
62	4 John.	*Simon son of Richer.	Roger son of Richer.
63	—	*Richard son of Ralph.	Bela de Freing by William her son.
64	—	*Matilda daughter of Godwin.	Boselinus de Brunham.
65	—	Vincent clericus de Surlingham.	*Herbert de Heloghetun.
66	—	*Godfrey son of Roger.	William de Burun.
67	—	Alan Walrain.	*Roger Bolle and Roger Dunewich.
67b	—	*John son of Alured.	Reginald son of Roger clericus, and John and Hugh his brothers.
68	—	Walter de Ravenigham.	*Robert . . . .
69	—	*Osbert de Lond and Agnes his wife.	John Lambert and Ailicē his wife.
70	—	*Nicholas son of Osbert.	William son of Geoffrey.
71	—	*Geoffrey son of John.	Richard son of Emeloc and Toke his brother.
72	—	*Tholy Wace.	Ranñ Capellanus.
73	—	*Werbald de Elingham.	Herland and Emma his wife.
74	—	Robert son of Torold.	*John de Norton.

Description of Property.	Consideration, &c.
Suldham, Fingham, Utwell, Surreia (?), Hilsingeton, Derham, and Reston.	
16 acres in Swaningeton.	The grant to Roger of ½ an acre in Swaningeton, which lies next the house of Hugh fil^y Wither, to hold by free service at 1^d yearly, for which Roger pays 10^s.
12 acres in Freing.	1 mark of silver.
10 acres in Brunham.	4 marks of silver.
22 acres in Surlingham for life of Ediva the mother of the said Vincent.	
5 acres in Freng.	The grant of 1 acre 1 rood in said town (. . . Medelesties) at 4^s a year.
⅓ acre in Hecham to hold at 1^d yearly.	4^s.
6 acres in Westwine.	1 mark of silver.
. . . . in Shelton. (Recites the grant to Walter de Suffield, in consideration of homage and 16 marks, of all his lands in Shelton, which he held in fee of Nicholas de Shelton . . . . . . to Olive his wife and William his son.)	40^s.
A piece of land, 16 feet broad and 60 feet long, in Len.	40^s sterling.
8 acres in Reinham.	A mark of silver.
12 acres in Gotele.	20^s of silver.
1 acre in Straton called Colescroft.	Half a mark.
10 acres in Elingham.	The grant of 3 acres in Elingham, viz., 1 acre in Crofto, 1 acre in Knapewellac^a, and 1 acre in Prestemere, to hold at 12¼^d yearly.
30 acres in Geistweie to hold by free service at 5^s yearly.	1 mark.

No.	Date.	"Petens."	"Tenens."
75	4 John.	Alan de Wicton.	*Richard son of Robert.
76	—	*William Carkene.	John son of Beatrix.
77	—	*Thomas son of Roger, and Geoffrey his brother, and Huelin their sister.	Richard Gerbald.
78	—	Herbert de Karletune.	*Roger Molendarius and Sibilla his wife.
79	—	John de Matlaske and Edith his wife.	*Lucā capellanus.
80	—	Godric Gerlag̃ and Esole his wife.	*Astiñ Reben and Matilda his wife.
81	—	Botilda daughter of Tony.	*Hugh son of William.
82	—	*Basil daughter of Ralph.	William son of Peter.
83	—	Alan de Wichtun.	*Roger de Cressingham and Agnes his wife.
84	—	Elvina daughter of Sugband (?) of Scriotbi (?)	Ralph son of Elfnoth and Elfleda his wife.
85	—	*Thoke and Godiva his wife	Geoffrey de Horseia.
86	—	Richard, Prior of the Holy Sepulchre of Thetford.	*William de Eston.
87	—	*Peter de Watling by Eborard clericus.	Lambert, Prior of Acre, by Richard janitor.

Description of Property.	Consideration, &c.
5 acres in Wicton.	The regrant of the eastern half at 8^d yearly.
3 acres in Swerdeston.	6^s sterling.
15 acres in Apet.	The regrant of 5 acres, viz., 1 acre 1 rood "ad Fredue," 3 roods at the head of the croft, 1 acre at Brome, and 1 acre 1 rood at Wadmar, $\frac{1}{2}$ an acre at Heued, and $\frac{1}{2}$ an acre at Dich, to hold at 15^d yearly.
2 acres in Carleton.	4^s and 6^d.
10 acres in Beremer, Berewic, and Stanho.	The regrant thereof to the said Luc and Paul his son and the heirs of the latter, to hold at 10^d yearly.
3 acres in Tilney, viz., 2 acres in Twisler in Neuloond of Tilnei and 1 acre in Sentford.	The regrant thereof to hold at 8^d yearly, and the payment by Godric of 20^s.
12 acres in Pagg^{a}ve.	Half a mark of silver.
30 acres in Wadtun.	One mark of silver.
Half a carucate in Wichtun.	10 marks.
7 acres in Ormesbi, of which the half towards the east, with the capital messuage thereon, was to remain to Ralph and Elfleda for their lives at free service, at 12^d yearly, and the other half to remain to Elvina and her heirs for ever, at 12^d yearly. After the death of Ralph and Elfleda, all the land to revert to Elvina.	
8 acres in Horseia.	3 marks of silver.
30 acres in Huningham and half a mill in Torp.	The regrant thereof to William and the heirs of his body at 7^d yearly.
60 acres in Lawendich and Diewude.	7^s rent in Marham, viz., of John Capellanus 2^s, of Robert ad Fontem 2^s 6^d, of Walter ad Fontem 1^s 6^d, and of William son of Reginald 1^s, to hold

No.	Date.	"Petens."	"Tenens."
88	4 John.	*Adā de Tisteshal.	Geoffrey son of Robert.
89	—	Thomas Blundus.	Lambert [Prior of Cast] ellacr̃.
90	—	William, parson of Helghetun.	*Godfry son of Alan.
91	—	*Gilbert son of Peter.	Richard son of Ivo and Richard de Clare and Agnes his wife.
92	—	*Richard Walēsern and Matilda his wife.	Roger son of Reginald.
93	—	*Geoffrey Crawe.	Raimer son of Robert and Walter his brother.
94	—	Herbert le Marchand and Mabil his wife.	William de Curcun.
95	—	*Lescia daughter of Reginald.	Roheis daughter of Reginald.

Description of Property.	Consideration, &c.
	by free service at the rent of a pound of cummin.
30 acres in Hargham.	1 mark of silver.
20 acres in Ruchhā, of which 8 acres, viz., ⅓ an acre in Akergate, 1 acre in Slokrundel, 2 acres in Katecroft .... super Evedlond de Katecroft, 1 acre in ...... 1½ acre abutting on Atterhill, and 2 acres in Grenegate abutting on Rigeweigate, should remain to the said Prior, and the remainder to the said Thomas to hold at 10ˢ yearly.	
Half an acre in Helghetun lying between Middelmilñ and the town of Helghetun.	
15 acres in Caldecote.	2 marks of silver.
4 acres in Freton.	10ˢ sterling.
30 acres in Stratun.	5 marks.
5 acres in Clipesbi, of which 4 should remain to Herbert and Mabil and the heirs of the latter, viz., 2⅓ acres in Dene, ⅓ an acre and ⅓ a rood towards the mill of Nicholas de Haledichs, 1⅓ rood under the wood of Richard de Clipesbi, and ⅓ an acre which Lawrence held in Manhondele, to hold at 6ᵈ yearly, and the remaining acre, which lies towards the north, should remain to William and his heirs, &c.	
Half a carucate in Ruieshal.	The regrant of 36 acres thereof, viz., 3 acres which were of Agnes Noreus, 4 acres which abutted on the way from Ruieshal to Puleham, 2 acres in Sandland, 2 acres in Northfield abutting on Estldefridding, 1½ acre at Snakesland, ⅓ an acre abutting on the meadow of Ruieshal, 2 acres in West Brakes, 11 acres

No.	Date.	"Petens."	"Tenens."
96	4 John.	*William Pens and Fulcho his brother.	Margaret de Cressingham.
97	—	*Hervey son of Eudo.	William son of Roscelin.
98	—	*Villiam [sic] Boisar.	Warin son of Ivo.
99	—	*Alured son of William.	Richard son of Robert.
100	—	*Philip son of Ivo.	Alan de Tivetshale.
101	—	*Cristiana daughter of Humfrey.	Richard son of Walter and Basilica his wife, and Matilda the latter's mother.
102	—	*Alice de Munpinzun.	Geoffrey de Assendon.
103	—	Henry son of Robert.	*Robert Faber and Botilda his wife.
104	—	*Martin son of Roger.	Peter son of Sirache.
105	—	Walter parson of Sweinestorp by Richard de Sweinestorp.	*Milo de Sweinestorp and Matilda his wife.
106	—	*Martin son of Roger.	Robert son of Athelward.

Description of Property.	Consideration, &c.
	lying eastwards from the mill, and 10 acres lying southwards from the mill, for which Roheise pays one mark of silver.
11 acres in Frawesham.	2^s sterling.
13 acres in Hemford.	1 mark of silver.
A messuage in Sumerton.	The grant of 1 rood in Sumerton next " toftrū putoc̃ " (? the well field) to hold at 2^d yearly.
30 acres in Claie.	Half a mark in silver.
60 acres in Tivetshale.	The grant of 6 acres in Tivetshale, at 6^d yearly, viz., 2 acres ad domum Scipard, ½ an acre ad boscum Piwith, 1½ acre at Bech, 2 acres at Rediz, and 2 acres which abut on the ditch at Muletun.
10 acres in Chineburdle.	32^s of silver.
28 acres in Wigenhale which are admitted to be of the right of Geoffrey and Margaret his wife, and the heirs of Margaret, to hold of Fulco de Munpinzun and his heirs by free service at 30^d yearly.	4 marks of silver. [Fulco was present and assented.]
7 acres in Freton.	5 marks of silver to Robert and Botilda, and 20^s and 10^s to Matilda and Alice the daughters of Botilda, who were present and released their rights.
3 acres in Westwineche.	Half a mark of silver.
10 acres in Sweinestorp in free alms to the Church of St. Peter of Sweinestorp.	2 marks of silver
7 acres in Westwinch.	23^s of silver.

No.	Date.	"Petens."	"Tenens."
107	4 John.	*John son of Walter and Roger his brother.	Richard son of William and Wlviva his wife.
108	—	*Ricard Toli.	Matilda vidua and William her son.
109	—	Haic (?) son of Turstan.	*Robert son of Edmund.
110	—	Thomas son of Henry.	*William de Nuiers and Thomas de Muntecorbyn.
111	—	Warin de Salle by Thomas son of Simon.	*Ralph de Nugguñ.
112	—	*Ralph son of Henry.	Agnes de Melham by John Pepĩ her son.
113	—	Nicholas de Halediz and Agnes his wife.	*William le Curcun of Clipesbi.
114	—	*Philip son of Yvo.	Geoffrey de Tiveteshall.
115	—	*Herbert son of Costion.	Paul de Mulkeberdeston.
116	—	*John and Robert sons of Ernald Burgo.	Reiner son of William.

Description of Property.	Consideration, &c.
Half a carucate in Iteringham.	2 marks of silver and the grant of 2 acres in the said town, viz., 1 acre called Hevedacre and 2 half acres at Two buskes (?) ad Wlng^{a}ve at 3^d yearly.
12 acres in Wiclewode.	The grant of 2 acres in the said town lying next at Morle at 4^d yearly.
Half a mill and 6 acres in Holte.	The regrant of half the mill and ½ a croft towards the west to the road, and 2½ acres upon Thingham, and ½ an acre at the King's mill, and ½ an acre at the Bridge mill, and ½ an acre in Exhaiz to hold by free service at 11^s 4^d yearly.
Half the advowson of the Church of St. Andrew of Wikelwod.	5 marks of silver.
6 acres in Corpesti.	The regrant thereof at 18^d yearly, for which Ralph pays 2^s of silver.
28 acres in Bittringe.	The grant of 1 acre next Lowedich towards the west to hold at 8^d yearly.
3 acres in Clipesbi (except the tenement of Robert capellanus of Billokesbi).	20^s sterling.
30 acres in Tiveteshal.	The grant of 2 acres in Tiveteshal called Ulnestuft at 2^d yearly; Geoffrey also pays half a mark of silver.
15 acres in Mulkeberdeston.	1 mark of silver.
2 carucates in Burgo and Adhelmerton.	The grant to Robert and his heirs by his then wife of 13 acres 3½ roods in campis de Burgo, viz., 5 acres ... 25 perches of the land which was of Stanard Cnappyng towards the west, 1 acre

No.	Date.	"Petens."	"Tenens."
117	4 John.	*Roger Caluñ.	John son of Beatrix.
118	—	*Robert son of Swan.	Reginald and Henry, sons of Roger.
119	—	*Roger son of Ralph.	Robert de Cree, and Robert son of Ralph and Alice his wife.
120	—	*Osbert de Schelfhangre.	Herbert son of Odo.
121	—	Inetta daughter of Godric.	*Thomas Dusing.
122	—	*Emma de Holme.	Robert de Hulme.
123	—	Roger de Bosco and Avelina his wife, and Helewin de Bosco and Mabil his wife.	*Roger fit Warin.
124	—	*Margaret fit William.	Wulfyat de Kattun.
125	—	*Martin de Saffrei.	Fulcher fit Richard.
126	—	*William fit Thomas.	Reginald fit Robert.
127	—	Ralph Abbot of Dierham.	*Peter fit Amund.
128	—	*Robert fit Helewin.	Hugh Capellanus by Stephen his brother.
129	—	*William de Massingeham.	William fit Herbert.
130	—	*John Withorspon and Sibil his wife, and Roger fit	Robert de Walton.

Description of Property.	Consideration, &c.
20 acres in Berton, 15 perches called Foxhole, 1 acre called ....., 5 acres 3½ roods of the land formerly of Ralph, &c.	The regrant of 1 acre thereof, viz., ½ acre at Allewellefen, between the land of William de Gimingham and the land of Nicholas parson, and ½ acre abutting on the Spinney at Allewellefen.
7 acres in Westwinch.	2 marks of silver.
7 acres in Fundchal.	The grant of 2½ acres in Fundchall, viz., in the croft of Wm. Brichtin.
30 acres in Lopham.	5 marks of silver.
10 acres in Sipeden.	20^s.
The reasonable dower of Emma in the free tenements which were of Robert de Hulme, in Hulme, Wicherestorp, Knardeston, Sudfeld, Bieston, Bradcham, Chilveston, Sutton, Cotes, and Gremeston.	The grant of one-third of all the lands which Robert, father of the said Robert de Hulme held in the same, "cum uno masag̃ qđ vocat^r vetɾ masag̃ de Hulme."
1½ acre in Nortun.	The regrant thereof at 8^d yearly, for which Roger pays half a mark.
8 acres in Kattun.	19^s sterling.
7 acres in S^{a}tton (Stratton?)	10^s sterling.
5 acres in Dr̃am (Dereham?)	1 mark of silver.
30 acres in Dierham.	4½ marks of silver.
2 acres of land and 1 toft in Winebotsham.	The regrant of the toft to Robert, to hold by free service at 4^d yearly, and the payment of 1 mark of silver to him.
12 acres in Massingeham.	The regrant thereof to Wm. de Massingeham and Ada his mother, to hold for their lives at 12^d yearly, for which regrant they pay 2 marks of silver.
A messuage in Lenn.	20^s sterling.

No.	Date.	"Petens."	"Tenens."
131	4 John.	Boselin and Salerna his wife. *Levina de Lenne.	The Prior of Ely by Roger the Monk.
132	—	*Robert fit William.	Geoffrey fit William.
133	—	*Botilda, niece of Wm. de Carleton, and Agnes and Avicia her sisters.	Adam de Dunham.
134	—	*Godfrey Pincerna.	Adam de Ho.
135	—	*John de Coletun.	Eleured Stein.
136	—	*William fit Ralph and Margaret his wife.	Ivo de Lincoln.
137	—	*Walter de Suffold and Oliva his wife.	Walter fit Roger.
138	—	William Osgot.	Thomas Busting.
139	—	*Reginald de Cornewall.	Ralph de M⁰lesham and Hawise his wife.
140	—	Henry Loholt.	*Alexander de Kirkeby by Wm. fit Roger.
141	—	Robert fit Roger.	*Blakeman Tot.
142	—	William fit Costar.	*Ralph Camararius.
143	—	*Goda daughter of Susan.	William Picot.
144	—	William fit Robert.	*William fit Godwin and Gilbert fit Rixxe (?)
145	—	*Roger Buzun.	Robert de Saham.

85

Description of Property.	Consideration, &c.
The reasonable dower of Levina, which she claims through William de Lenn, her late husband.	2 marks of silver.
16 acres in Burston.	3 marks of silver.
10 acres in Carleton.	6 marks of silver.
20 acres in Hindringham.	20ˢ sterling.
6 acres in Coletun.	The regrant of 2 acres thereof, viz., 1 acre at Bereford Mill towards the east, and 1 acre at Langeroe, to hold by free service at 8ᵈ yearly.
A messuage in Lenn.	20ˢ sterling.
The reasonable dower of Oliva as widow of Roger fit Walter, her late husband, in Raveningham and Norcot.	30 marks of silver.
2 acres in Grovele (?)	A partition by which Wm. took the north and Thos. the south half.
50 (?) acres in Burnhamtorp.	½ mark of silver.
10 acres "de alneto" (alder carr?) in Eligham and in Mickelfen.	The regrant to Alexander at the yearly rent of a pound of pepper.
"De t͞ib͞ȝ dim̃ acr͞ ͡tre" in Hueton.	The regrant of the western half at 4ᵈ yearly.
1½ acre in Sotesham (Shotesham ? or Totesholm.—Vide Bl. *Norf.* i., p. 498.)	2ˢ of silver.
6 acres in .... and	The grant of 2 acres, viz., 1 acre which abutted on the road next William's mill, ½ acre on the same road, and ½ acre on Haxland, at 2ᵈ yearly.
4 acres in Wichingham.	The grant of 1 acre, which Warin held, at 8ᵈ yearly.
A carucate of land in Uvinton (Ovington) and Kerebroc.	The regrant of 16 acres and a messuage in Uvinton,

No.	Date.	"Petens."	"Tenens."
146	4 John.	Ulf Luvel and Lecia his wife.	*Thomas de Ingollesthorp and Matilda his mother.
147	—	Petronilla de Mortuo Mari by Walter fit Robert.	*William de Bukcham.
148	—	*Robert fit Peter.	Semann fit Robert.
149	—	Henry Bacun.	*Roger Bacun.
150	—	*Roger Gloz.	Richard Gloz.
151	—	*John Le Sire.	Herbert, Prior of Kokesford, by Hervey fit Walter.
152	—	*Adam fit Walter.	Walter le ......
153	—	*Godwin fit Goscelin and Emma his wife.	Godfrey, Mabil, Estonild, and Sumered.
154	—	*John fit Thede.	Roger fit Turstan.
155	—	*Simon de Inlande.	Goscelin de Bronn (vel Broun) and Alienor his wife.

Description of Property.	Consideration, &c.
	viz., 6½ acres at Langeland, 10 acres in Grasecroft, and a messuage, which Thurkill held, at 18^d yearly.
5 acres in Snetesham.	The regrant to Thos. and Matilda and the heirs of Thomas, to hold at 6^d yearly, they paying 10^s sterling for the same.
20 acres, &c., in Bukēham, and the advowson of the church of Old	The release of all rights over the 20 acres, excepting to her and her heirs "trib⁊ bodis (rodis?) scilicet in Calculnes-howe."
17 acres in Houton.	Half a mark of silver.
Half a mark of rent in Cherwelleston, to hold at service of four barbed arrows.	A hawk.
20 acres in	The regrant of 1½ acre, lying next Stanhoegate, next the land of Richard fit S . . . . .
24 acres in Frenges.	20^s sterling and the yearly rent of a pound of pepper, or 6^d.
4 acres in Walsokē.	2 marks of silver.
3 acres of land and 3 acres of wood in Ilsington.	The regrant of 1½ acre thereof, viz., 3 roods between the land of the church of Ilsingtun and 3 roods between the land of St. Edmund and the land of Robert de Chevervill.
2 acres in Seche.	3 marks of silver.
17 acres in Inland and Gatele.	2 marks of silver and the release to Simon of an acre and a half and a rood and a half in Inland next his house, in exchange for which last-mentioned ground Simon grants to Goscelin and

No.	Date.	"Petens."	"Tenens."
156	4 John.	*Stephen fil Godwin.	Clement and Roger de Coleby and Alviva their mother.
157	—	Stannard fil Hulf.	*Gunilda fil Hervei.
158	—	*Philip fil Yvo.	William fil Yvo.
159	—	*Thomas fil Safrid.	Robert Estrun (?)
160	—	*Ralph de Boilund.	Geoffrey de Lagetoft (*sic* Langetoft ?)
161	—	*William de Fossato.	Thomas fil Nichol.
162	—	*Selvestr̃ de Winebotesham.	Estmund fil Suneman.
163	—	*Peter Molendinar and Thurgand his wife.	Ralph clericus.

Description of Property.	Consideration, &c.
	wife 2 acres in the same town, abutting on the fee of the Hospital of Jerusalem.
6 acres in Coleby.	The grant of an acre in the same town, of which half was in the field called Kenting welle [or Kemingwelle] and the other between the land of Simon de Krakeford and Simon fil Ralph at Colebythorn, to hold at a penny yearly.
A messuage in Herdelay	The regrant thereof, with half the marsh which belonged thereto and lay to the west, to hold for her life.
30 acres in Tivetshal.	The grant of 2 acres in Tivetshal which is next Ulnestuft [or Ulvestuft] to hold at 2^d yearly and the payment to Philip of 2 marks of silver.
3s. rent in Stratun.	2 marks of silver.
30 acres in Saxlingeham and Thurmodetun.	1 mark of silver.
A carucate in Karletun.	5^s rent in Dalling receivable as follows, from Stanard Witing and his heirs 15^d; from Braies the wife of Robert and his heirs 15^d; from Beatrix the mother of Hugh 15^d; and from Hugh the son of Turkill and his heirs 15^d.
12 acres in Wincbotesham.	6^s sterling.
24 acres in Mundeford.	The grant of 6 acres in the same town, viz., 3 roods sub Cranewissegat, 1 rood subter Cranewissegat, 1 rood at the church, 3 roods subter Feltwellegat,

No.	Date.	"Petens."	"Tenens."
164	4 John.	Adam de Vallibʒ.	*Oliver de Vallibʒ.
165	—	Bartholomew Faber.	*Richard de Bernyngham.
166	—	Cristiana fit Hugh.	*Hugh de Dunestun.
167	—	Gilbert, Abbot of Langeleia.	*Roeisia fit Reginald de Ruieshal.
168	—	Durant de Argentis and Roeisin his wife, and Simon de Waletun.	*Nicholas de Walesham.
169	—	*Peter fit Siric.	William Steingrūn (Steingrim?)

Description of Property.	Consideration, &c.
	1 acre and 1 rood in Swersland, 3 roods near Wetingate merr, 3 roods abutting 'ad linesti,' 1 acre upon Stanberh, and 1½ rood next Wetigat, to hold at 6ᵈ yearly.
2 carucates in Chedestane.	The regrant thereof to Oliver for his life.
6 acres in Dalling.	The regrant thereof to hold at 22ᵈ yearly, for which regrant Richard pays 20ˢ sterling.
3½ acres in Dunestun.	The yearly rent of 14ᵈ.
41 acres in Ruieshal.	5 marks of silver and the yearly rent of 3ˢ.
A fishery in Thillebiŕ. *	The regrant of the fishery "et I fluetto qⁱ vocatʳ Alfladeflet ⁊ sitˢ I molendūn sup eūd fluct ubicq̧, Nicño voluit molend illđ constituere ⁊ I chimiñ qⁱerit ī Latitudine" of 24 feet, extending in length from the house of Salomon the Carpenter to "Tamisiā," to hold at 3ˢ yearly, for which regrant Nichᵒ pays 9ˢ sterling.
20 acres in Lenn and West Winn3.	The grant to Peter by William of all his lands in the marsh of Lenn lying between the fee of the Prior of Acre towards the north, and the fee of the Lord of Westweni3, &c., of a rod of land next the croft of Simon le Neweman, &c., to hold at 2ˢ yearly, for all which Peter pays 10ˢ sterling.

* This would seem to relate to Tilbury near Gravesend, from the reference to the Thames, and it is difficult to see why it is found among the Norfolk fines.

No.	Date.	"Petens."	"Tenens."
170	4 John.	Agnes Gñte, by John her son.	*John de Warples, John de Eggemere, and Matthew de Waterden.
171	—	Bartholomew de Brandon and Bartholomew (*sic*) his brother.	*John fil .... (torn)
172	—	*Geoffrey Crawe.	Roger de S^{a}tton (Stratton?)
173	—	Basil fil Swartagar.	*Edwin Carpenter.
174	—	*Joscelin de Birlingham and Matilda his wife, William and Margaret his wife, John de Depeham and Isabel his wife, and Emma their sister.	Geoffrey de Amblie.
175	—	*Richard Mercator and Alice his wife.	Richard Trenebury and Mabel his wife, and Basilia her mother.
176	—	*Ralph Hille.	Herveus son of Roger.
177	—	*John de Coletun.	William Brun.
178	—	*Andrew de Couteshal.	William son of Hervey.
179	—	*Elveva daughter of Alured.	Gervase and Nicholas de Filebi.
180	—	Robert Mautalent.	John, Alexander, and Thomas, the sons of Leswin.

Description of Property.	Consideration, &c.
Reasonable dower in . . . . . . from the gift of Ralph Grante her late husband.	The regrant thereof at 8^d yearly.
An acre in Bernham.	The yearly rent of 3^d.
40 acres in Stratton.	40^s sterling and the grant of 18 acres in Stratton which Geoffrey held of Roger at 2^s yearly.
$3\frac{1}{2}$ acres in Massingeham.	No consideration mentioned.
Half a knight's fee in Beghetun.	20 marks of silver.
40 acres in Berncham.	2 marks of silver.
18 acres in Bitringe. (†) $4\frac{1}{2}$ acres in Herolfvesrode and $4\frac{1}{2}$ acres in Kirkegate Way.	The regrant of 9 acres part thereof, viz., (†) to hold by free service at 6^d yearly.
6 acres in Coletun. (†) 1 acre at the mill of Bereford.	The regrant of (†) to hold by free service at 4^d yearly.
22 acres in Fretenham.	30^s sterling.
$5\frac{1}{2}$ acres in Filebi.	16^s sterling.
Agreement as to $\frac{1}{3}$ one virgate and $\frac{1}{3}$ of another $\frac{1}{3}$ virgate in Walsokne, viz., that one quarter thereof with the services of Achard and Goding should remain to "the aforesaid church" (no church is mentioned in any part of the fine), and the remaining three quarters should remain to the said John Alexander and Thomas to hold of the said church by free service at 12^d yearly.	

No.	Date.	"Petens."	"Tenens."
181	4 John.	Ralph son of Alegar.	Alan son of Ailmar.
182	—	*Alan nephew of Wulfric.	Roger son of Ralph.
183	—	*Alice daughter of Hakun de Bernham.	Matthew and Leuiñ (Levina?) his wife.
184	—	Roger Dulle.	*Roger son of Gocelin.
185	—	*Walter son of Edrich.	Henry de Fleg and Ralph H'dwan.
186	—	*Henry de Habetun.	Henry le Puillicis de Brisingham.
187	—	*William de la leg.	William son of Richard.
188	—	*William Glauie.	Ingeleth fil' Lefwin.
189	—	Earl Roger Le Bigod.	*Robert de Cree and Agnes his wife.
190	—	Luke de Hille and Matilda his wife, and William de Hil and Briethua his wife.	*Margaret the widow and Adam her son.
191	—	*William de Bukeham.	Nigell de Stamford.
192	—	Osbert de Wachesham.	*William de Estoñ.
193	—	Roger son of Morand.	*Ralph son of Arnild.
194	—	*Editha and Botilda her sister.	William son of Fredoñ.
195	—	*Edmund son of Robert.	David de Houtun.

Description of Property.	Consideration, &c.
11 acres in Torp and Stratton. (†) 3 acres 1 rood in Torp and Stratton, viz., at Cockesseğ, Selomere, Selimere (?) and Grenestic.	The grant in exchange of (†).
18 acres in B^ytun (Barton).	2 marks of silver.
15 acres in Bernham.	5ˢ of silver.
5 acres in Karkebi.	2 marks of silver.
6 acres in Waxtonesham.	15ˢ of silver.
24 acres in Brisingham.	30ˢ.
5 acres in Karleton.	3½ marks of silver.
8 acres and 1 messuage in Tilney.	30ˢ sterling.
20ˢ of land (sic) in Coleby.	40 marks of silver.
4 acres in Nereford (†) 3 acres thereof, viz., at Abunesgate, at Marlingate, at Didelstie, at Yotenden, and at Burgdich.	The regrant of (†) to hold by free service at 2½ᵈ yearly.
The advowson of the church of Bukeham.	4 marks of silver.
20 acres in Eston, Coleton, and Nlingeford.	The regrant of the whole to hold by free service at 2ˢ yearly.
4 acres in Ringsted.	The yearly payment of 6ᵈ.
24 acres in Erwelestun. (†) Half thereof, viz., in Crophto, in Hafketelestofta, at the house of Godd, at Humstie, at Suthewelle, at Estgate, at Chirchegat, at Onecoteshed, at Wilgeshik, at Gilbert's land, at Benehalfacre, at Schortchalfacre, which abuts on Brechegate, at Edwinestoft, at Schorteland, "ad capud Parchi," under Linghil, abutting on Beeslade, and under Fredeswude. (‡) 1 acre in Erwelestun after the death of Emma the mother of the said Editha and Botilda, which she lately held of the said William in dower.	The regrant of (†) to hold by free service at 6ᵈ yearly, and the grant of (‡) to hold at 1ᵈ yearly.
14 acres in Houton. (†) An acre in Houton, half at Broccross and half "sub cur Edmundi."	The grant of (†) to hold at 4ˢ yearly and the cash payment of 8ˢ sterling.

No.	Date.	" Petens."	" Tenens."
196	4 John.	Walter de Raveningham.	*Cecilia de Nortun.
197	—	*Bartholomew de Reddam.	William son of Matthew de Reddham.
198	—	Richard Pulein by William his brother.	Godard son of Edric.
199	—	*William and John and Robert his brothers.	Brogo son of Godfrey de Reinham.
200	—	*Ranulph the son of Howard.	Emma de Saxlingham.
201	—	*William son of Thomas.	Alan the Chaplain.
202	—	*Hugelina daughter of Godwin.	Aubert son of Bonde.
203	—	*Elfer and Alice his wife.	Philip Prior of Acre.
204	—	*William Clerenbaud.	Roger magister de Simplingham by John Buistard (sic) his attorney.
205	—	*Richard Pulein.	William de Hill and Goda his wife.
206	—	John de Beremer and Emma his wife.	*Luke the Chaplain.
207	—	Godard son of Toni.	Henry son of Godwin and Stephen his brother.
208	—	*Wimar son of William.	Richard son of Simon.

Description of Property.	Consideration, &c.
A marsh in Norton and 15 acres in Lodne. This fine is a warranty of a charter (therein set out) by which Cecilia, daughter of Cristian de Norton, grants to Walter de Sudfeld, in consideration of his homage and 100ˢ, all her inheritance in Lodne which was of the fee of Goscelin de Lodnes, viz., Milnehoe mersh, to hold to him and Olive his wife and William his son and their heirs, at 6ᵈ yearly.	40ˢ sterling.
5ˢ rent in Whittun.	The regrant of (†) at the yearly rent of a pound of pepper.
(†) The site of the mill and mill pool of Whittun.	
30 acres in Horstun.	The equal division thereof.
32 acres in Reinham.	The regrant of (†) to hold at 14ᵈ yearly.
(†) 10 acres thereof, viz., under the .... of John Pauper, at Hevekeshill, in Estmore, at Nungate, at Bergate, at Suthwadhēgat and at Stanaue.	
9 acres in Saxlingham.	1 mark of silver.
3 acres in Brom.	1 mark of silver.
Half a messuage in Lenn.	40ˢ sterling.
40 acres in Harīgeshāg.	40ˢ sterling.
15 acres in Welles to hold to the said Roger and his successors.	30ˢ sterling and participation in the benefits, &c., of the said house of Simplingham for ever.
18 acres in Horstede.	6ˢ sterling.
10 acres in Beremere, Berewie, and Stanho.	The regrant thereof to Luke and his son Paul and his heirs, to hold of John and Emma and their heirs by free service at 12ᵈ yearly, &c.
1 acre in Mothetun (Moulton.)	An equal division.
60 acres in Quidēham.	The regrant thereof to hold by the free service of a pound of pepper annually and scutage.

No.	Date.	"Petens."	"Tenens."
209	4 John.	*Geoffrey the Chaplain.	Roger son of Safrid.
210	—	John de Muncorbin.	*Geoffrey son of David.
211	—	*Warner de Waxtunesham.	Vincent Prior of Thetford.
212	—	*Alan de Snitertone and Alice his wife.	Nicolas son of Philip.
213	—	*William son of Emma.	Warin de Aldehage.
214	—	Mabilia daughter of William de Bretheham and Adeldreda her sister.	*Walter fit Hervey and James his brother.
215	—	*Richard de Senges by Robert le Gris.	Roger de Ho.
216	—	Roger Kempe and Margaret his wife, and Ulfketell of Derby and Hawise his wife, and Eda the widow.	William fit Merild.

Description of Property.	Consideration, &c.
3 acres in Burstone.	Half a mark of silver.
3 acres in Bernham.	The regrant thereof to hold by free service at 16ᵈ yearly.
2 carucates in Kilverdestun "et de Norewika cum ptin," and the service of Damia (?) in Croxtun, viz., 4ᵈ and a fishery in Snareshill worth 5ˢ, and the meadow of Henundesholm (?)	(*a*) The grant to Warner of all his fee in Thorp and Heveringham in homage, rent, and other services, to hold for ever at the free service of a pound of incense yearly ; (*b*) mutual releases of all claims ; and (*c*) the payment to Warner of 100 marks of silver.
40 acres in Birlingham and Pankesford. (†) 14 acres in the same places, viz., at Brendeland, Kinesmannestoft, Blakeland, at the land of William Leffta, and in the turbary in Pankessford next to the turbary of Geoffrey de Sisseslc.	The grant of (†) to hold at the yearly service of 22ᵈ.
6 acres in Toftes. (†) 1 acre in Toftes lying at Twelfacres.	The grant of (†) to hold by free service at 1ᵈ yearly, Warin paying 1 mark of silver.
20 acres in Bretham and all other land which said William Bretham held.	The regrant of 20 acres in the same town which Matilda the mother of the said Walter and James held in dower with her house after her death, viz., 14 acres next the land of Lineč, and 6 acres in Lingmiddelberg̃ to hold at 2ᵈ yearly.
12 acres in Topecroft in Wudetun.	4 marks of silver.
5 acres in Bilneia.	An equal division.

No.	Date.	"Petens."	"Tenens."
217	4 John.	*Margaret daughter of William.	Alan de Bassingeb'ue.
218	—	William fit Godric.	Basil de Stibde and Henry his son.
219	—	Reginald Bulax.	Stephen Bulax, Nigel de Bifeld, Geoffrey Portar, and Robert fit Richard.
220	—	*Gaufridus fit Alice.	William de Rakeia and Amabilia his mother.
221	—	*Thomas de Redham.	Wimer his brother.
222	—	*Ralph de Dalling.	.... Prior of Binham and Reginald Chaplain of Little Riburg.
223	—	*Ralph son of Godwin.	William Turnel.
224	—	*Alice daughter of William de Hadestune.	Agatha her sister.
225	—	*Helias son of Ralph.	Wido de Torp.

Description of Property.	Consideration, &c.
14 acres in Thorpe.	The regrant to her at 2ˢ and 1 lb. of pepper a year, for which regrant she pays 2 marks of silver.
6½ acres in Stiberde.	An equal division.
2ˢ rent in Wimundham and Wramplingham.	Ditto.
One-third of a carucate in Rakeia.	2 marks of silver.
35 acres in Redham.	24 acres in Redham and Limpenhoch, viz., 14 acres which Ketel de Skaft held, 2 acres in Hacheneseroft, 2 acres at the gate of Peter de Hill, 1 acre at Hildikesende, 1 acre at Roulond (or Rotilond) 1 acre at Bertigrave, 2 acres at Hestecroft, and 1 acre at Liteling; also the marsh which their father Roger held between Merestlet and Hildelf; also Agnes, dau. of Segviun (?) with all her holding & following: to hold at 3ˢ 3ᵈ yearly.
10 acres in Parva Riburg.	10ˢ.
24 acres in Rakeie.	Half a mark of silver.
A fourth part of the lands of the said William in Lyneste, Carletone Rode, and Tibenham (?)	... marks of silver.
4ˢ 6ᵈ rent in Meregetᵒp.	4 acres in Herwic in augmentation of the free tenement which he held of the petent in Rugunchac which lies next the croft of Waringer Frost.

No.	Date.	"Petens."	"Tenens."
226	4 John.	Otewie de Clipestorp.	*Roger Viere.
227	—	*Cristina daughter of Pagan.	Geoffrey son of William.
228	—	Robert Abbot of Ramesia.	*William le Curteis. [N.B. "Rich^d le Curteis apponuit clamam suam."]
229	—	Turkil son of Richard.	Stephen de Caldecote.
230	—	John de Depeham and Isabel his wife.	*Joscelin de Birlingham and Matilda his wife.
231	—	John de Reinestorp.	*Roger fit William by William fit Roscelin his his attorney.
232	—	Robert de Titeleshal.	*Alan fit Robert.
233	—	*Stephen fit Peter.	Miles fit Simon.
234	—	Berthol' Clerk and Berthol' Palmer.	*Richard de Baifeld.
235	—	*Jocelin de Lewes.	Hugh de Monasterio by Godefridus Colebee his attorney.
236	—	*Emma de Herpelay.	Matthew de Gurnay.

Description of Property.	Consideration, &c.
1 acre in Clipestorp.	The regrant at 4^d yearly, Roger paying 3^s sterling.
Half an acre in Gatesle.	6^s sterling.
20 acres in Welles, and the quit claim of 15 acres in Welles which lie within the old fee.	The regrant of such land and all other land which Walter the father of the said William held in Welles and Emeneth and Heligeia, and elsewhere, on the day he went to Jerusalem, to hold at 20^s and 6200 sticks of eels yearly.
5 acres in Oxeburg.	18^s sterling.
12 acres in Birlingham.	The regrant for the lives of Goscelin and Matilda at 4^s a year, for which regrant they pay 5 marks of silver.
One-sixth part of a mill in Taseburg.	Half a mark of silver.
Half a carucate in Titleshal.	The regrant of 10 acres, viz., 3$\frac{1}{2}$ at Holegate (which were of Reiner le Gay), 2$\frac{1}{2}$ at Treisdikes, 1 at Colput, 1 acre at Greiputtes, 1 at Aslakebusk (next the land of Hugh fit Hulf), and 1 in Sirmecopt (?) to hold at 12^d yearly.
1 carucate of land in [torn away.]	20^s sterling.
Half the advowson of Brandon.	100^s sterling.
14 acres in Heacham.	30^s sterling.
20 acres in Herpelay.	The regrant of 2$\frac{1}{2}$ acres, viz., 1 at Piggescroft and 1$\frac{1}{2}$ at Kaimluesmerchevedland at 6^d rent.

No.	Date.	"Petens."	"Tenens."
237	4 John.	*Walter fit Edrith.	Wimar Carpentarius.
238	—	*Ralph fit Mauger.	Thomas de Banīgham.
239	—	Adam fit Robert.	*Thomas fit Edward
240	—	Robert de Suthdale by Simon his son.	*John fit Robert.
241	—	*John Gret (or Grei?)	Simon le Newoman.
242	—	*William de Baduent by Robert de Craneford.	Walter fit Thurstan.
243	—	Alfwin Stalun and Goda his wife.	*John fit Baldwin.
244	—	*Robert de Bodham.	Lefwin de Bodham.
245	—	*Matilda daughter of Semar.	Odo and William sons of Herbert.
246	—	*Martin fit Adam.	Safred de Rungetun.
247	—	*Godwin fit Thurstan.	Simon fit Robert.
248	—	*Julian fit Bunde.	Richard fit Reginald.
249	—	Robert fit Hugh.	Philip fit Geoffrey.
250	—	*Robert de Vaus by William fit Peter.	Ralph Abbot of Hulm.
251	—	*Geoffrey de Randeworth.	Stephen fit Thomas.

Description of Property.	Consideration, &c.
8 acres in Waxtonesham.	1 mark of silver.
18 acres in Baningham.	12^s sterling.
10 acres in Bramertun.	2^s sterling.
22 acres in Plumstede and B^{o}nigham and Wītune.	8 acres in a field called Westwude to hold at 26^d rent.
10 acres in Westwenich.	9^s sterling.
One-fourth part of a knight's fee in Stikingeland.	100^s sterling.
9½ acres in Sweinestorp.	Regrant of 3 acres thereof which were of the fee of Hubert de Broc, and 3^s sterling.
1 acre in Bodham.	The grant to Elyas de Bodham of 1 acre in same town in a field called Wileghes to hold at 6^d rent.
9½ acres of land and ⅓ acre of meadow in Morlay.	Grant of 1 acre in same town, viz., 3 roods at Langeland and 1 rood at Trendele to hold at 2^d rent. Odo and William also give a bullock.
2½ acres in Sieche.	1 mark of silver.
10 acres in Lenne.	20^s sterling.
6 acres in Becham.	1 mark of silver.
1 messuage and 8 acres in Burnham. A partition whereby Robert receives 4 acres and the homage of Ade fit Edwine, viz., 2 acres in Litleholgat and 1 acre in the croft of Symon and 1 acre beyond the house of Walkelin de Rosetto, and Philip receives (†)	(†) 4 acres with the capital messuage, to hold by free service, viz., by soccage to the king at 1 mark and 5^d yearly.
2 carucates in Scotesham.	4 acres in Scotesham (which Robert, father of the said Robert de Vaus, gave to the church of St. Benedict of Hulm) and 30 marks sterling.
15 acres in Walesham.	The regrant to hold at 2^s and seven quarters of . . . yearly.

No.	Date.	" Petens."	" Tenens."
252	4 John.	Godwin fit Hugh.	*Baldwin de Lius (?) and Matilda his wife.
253	—	*Robert de Sutton and Alice his wife by Alured de la Gare their attorney.	Hugh de Horleberge.
254	—	Peter de Norfolk.	*Bartholomew de Walsingham.
255	—	*Bartholomew Faber.	William fit Elye.
256	—	*John fit Ralph.	Ralph de Dallinge.
257	—	Richard de Rumulli.	*Alice de Manerio.
258	—	William fit Asketel.	*Richard fit Bonde.
259	—	Armeniard fit Edric.	*Godwin fit Turstan.
260	—	William fit Umfr'.	*Warin de Aldehage.
261	—	*William fit William.	William Palmar.
262	—	*Gerard Prior of the Holy Trinity of Norwich.	Thomas fit Walter Decañ.
263	—	Ralph Abbot of Hulm.	*Thomas Ridell and Cecilia his wife.
264	—	*Ordwi (?) or Cyrdwi (?) fit Roger.	Henry fit William and Roger fit Ode.
265	—	*Hugh fit Roger.	Rœsia fit Reginald.
266	—	William Chaplain of Tortun.	*Matilda fit Torald.
267	—	*Bartholomew fit Walter.	Simon his brother.
268	—	*Gaufrid fit William.	William de Eston.
269	5 John.	*Peter de Glocc (?)	Alan de Hakebeche.
270	—	Walter de Creping.	*Ralph fit Siredd'.

Description of Property.	Consideration, &c.
2 acres in Wichingham.	12^d of silver.
A knight's fee in Prilleston.	10 marks of silver.
40 acres in Walsingham.	The regrant for life at a rent of 1 mark of silver a year.
4 acres in Dallinge.	Half a mark of silver.
8 acres in Parva Riburg.	The regrant of the western half at 12^d yearly.
Half a virgate in Wicclesford.	The yearly rent of 6^d.
7 acres in Cree.	4^s of silver.
Half of 3 messuages and 5 acres in Fotestone.	2^s sterling.
6 acres in Tofta.	40^s sterling.
5 acres in Filebi.	Half an acre " in campo de Filebi apud Poketorp," and ½ a mark of silver.
36¾ acres of land, 4½ acres of wood and pasture, and 4¼ acres of meadow in Tisteshal.	The grant to the Prior of 5½ acres in Tisteshal which Dana fit Walteri held of the Prior.
One-third of the advowson of Bastwic.	Half a mark of silver.
7 acres in Wikingham.	20^s sterling.
A carucate in Ruieshal.	4 marks of silver.
6 acres in Carleton which she held of the fee of Herbert de Helegton, viz., 2 in Albecroft, ½ which Bricce Biscop held, 3 roods lying at Suthill, ½ before the gate of W^m. Job, ½ at Asgereshill, ½ abutting on ditto, and ½ next Hescogate.	10^s sterling and 8^d yearly rent. [The fine sets out her charter at length.]
"De iiij^{or}xx^{te} ac$\bar{r}$ $\bar{r}$re et de x cum ptin$\bar{e}$cis in Asle." (? 90 acres.)	The grant of 23 acres thereof to hold of Simon at 42^d yearly.
.... in M ... ingford and Carleton.	All the land of the said William in Karleton to hold at 3^s yearly.
The advowson of Sauton.	3^s sterling.
12 acres in Eligham.	The regrant at 2^s yearly rent, for which regrant he pays a mark of silver.

No.	Date.	"Petens."	"Tenens."
271	5 John.	*Levena widow of William fit Costentin.	Ralph de Brecham.
272	—	Alexander Prior of Hickling by Augustin the Canon.	*Henry de Fleg.
273	—	William de Warenn.	*Haco de Well.
274	—	*Estilda (?) widow of Richard fit Torald.	William fit Richard.
275	—	William de Warenn.	.... Bude (? Bunde.)
276	—	*Ralph de Curzun.	Geoffrey de Marisco.
277	—	Warin Oisel and Beatrice his wife by Simon fit Robert.	*William fit Richard.
278	—	*Elyas fit Richard.	Henry de Bosco.
279	—	John Bishop of Norwich.	*Hamo fit Burdi.
280	—	(Illegible.)	Juliana .....
281	—	*Hubert fit Alexander.	Goscelin de Walpol.
282	—	Ralph fit Peter.	*Walter fit Umfrey.
283	—	Eborard Clericus.	Alexander de Yole.
284	—	(Illegible.)	
285	—	Alan de Hockeringham.	*Hubert de Rochage.
286	—	*Christina daughter of Leofwin by Simon de Howe.	Matilda de Bekeswelle by Robert Heron.
287	—	*Adam de Wesenham and Basilia his wife.	Ralph Abbot of Derham.

Description of Property.	Consideration, &c.
Her dower in Lenn and West Weniz.	10^s.
The advowson of Waxtonesham.	The grant by Theobald de Valones "advocatus domus de Hikeling" to Henry of all the land he held of him in Sumerton, Winterton, &c.
7½ acres in Well.	The regrant at 9^d yearly rent, for which regrant Hacho pays ½ a mark of silver.
.... Gontyñg.	(Illegible.)
.... Welles.	(Illegible.)
A carucate of land and a mill in Hechamthorp.	5 marks of silver.
A messuage in Lenn.	The regrant at 12^d yearly rent, for which regrant William pays 7 marks of silver.
A carucate in Bodham.	10 acres which William Sacerdos of Bernyngham held, and a mark of silver.
Common of pasture in Horningetoft.	The regrant at 2^s yearly rent.
(Illegible.)	(Illegible.)
A messuage in Lenn which belonged to Hubert the uncle of the said Hubert.	20 marks of silver. [This fine is made with the consent of William, Geoffrey, and Hamo, the brothers of the said Hubert.]
20 acres in Banham.	The regrant at 3^s 2^d yearly rent and 5½ marks of silver.
.... Winebodesham.	(Illegible.)
16 acres in	(Illegible.)
16 acres in Bekeswelle.	40^s.
23 acres in Tilney.	5 marks of silver.

No.	Date.	"Petens."	"Tenens."
288	5 John.	William de Warenn.	*(Illegible.)
289	—	*Alexander fit William.	Richer fit William.
290	—	..... widow of Wm. fit Costenton.	Thiedric Est . seon of Lenn.
291	—	Roger de Stratton.	Ranulph fit Robert.
292	6 John.	Richard fit Nicholas.	Adam fit Wido.
293	—	Wm. Prior of Norwich.	(Illegible.)
294	—	Alexander de Pole.	*Robert fit Ralph.
295	—	(Illegible.)	William de Warham.
296	—	*Stephen fit Bartholomew.	Thomas Prior of .... by Laurence de Thebrigg.
297	—	(Illegible.)	
298	—	*Beatrix fit Wulric and Ediva her sister by Wm. de Eford.	Roger de Norwic.
299	—	*Walter fit Roger.	Robert de Mortemer.
300	—	*John Marescall and .... his wife by Simon de Liclington.	The Prior of the Blessed Mary of Sudwark.
301	—	*Juliana widow of Ralph Clericus.	William le Gros.
302	—	*Walter son of Roger de Bilneia by Alexander de Ormesby his attorney.	Richard de Scinges.
303	—	Ralph Prior of Dunmawe.	*Hugh fit Odo.
304	—	Roger fit Gilbert.	*Herbert de Helgheton.
305	—	*Estrilda, Mazeline, and Alice, daughters of Ilingi.	Simon Master of the Hospital of .... of Norwich.
306	—	(Illegible.)	John Clericus of Dalling.

Description of Property.	Consideration, &c.
7½ acres in Well.	Half a mark of silver.
A carucate of land in Timethorp and Refham.	The grant to Alexander of 3 acres in Timethorp abutting on a messuage which was of Simon his grandfather.
Dower in West Weniz.	(Illegible.)
(Illegible.)	(Illegible.)
.... Twai.	
.... in suburb of Norwich.	(Illegible.)
12 acres in Wimbodesham.	The regrant to hold of Eborard fit Baldewin. Eborard pays half a mark.
(Illegible.)	
2 messuages in Lenna and 36 acres in Walsingham.	The regrant to Stephen of the Walsingham land.
18 acres in Tacolneston.	20^s.
Advowson of Raveningham.	The grant of the homage and soccage of Walter de Sudfeld.
Advowsons of Hogring and Berk.	(Illegible.)
30 acres in Betele.	10^s.
A carucate in Grimestun.	20 marks of silver.
16 acres in Hemehale.	14^d yearly. Robert fit Walter, lord of the fee, is mentioned.
30^s in rent in Karleton.	40^s.
1 acre in Katton.	8^s sterling.
40 acres in Dalling, being a grant to Roger Bacon and his heirs to hold of the said John and Peter his son.	(Illegible.)

112

No.	Date.	"Petens."	"Tenens."
307	6 John.	*Richard son of Mabel.	William Russu.
308	—	Magister William de Lenn by Roger de Norwich his attorney.	*Livena de Walesham by Geoffrey de Norwich, her attorney.
309	—	William Abbot of Sa .. e.	(Illegible.)
310	—	*William fit Richard.	Richard Noth.
311	—	(Illegible.)	
312	—	Rauñ the brother of Goucy by Ralph de Hemsted.	*Geoffrey fit Ailward.
313	7 John.	*Adam Clericus of Dalling.	Roger de Dalling by Ralph his son.
314	—	John del Frith.	*Lecia fit Ralph and Emma her daughter by Ralph del Frith.
315	—	*(Illegible.)	Alexander de Jernemue.
316	—	Magister Ralph Bacun (?)	*William de Hulmo.
317	—	*Ralph de Beufo.	Philip Prior of Estacre.
318	—	Richard de Ho.	Luke Sacerdos and Elyas his son.
319	—	(Illegible.)	(Illegible.)
320	—.	*Ralph de Tirinton.	Magister Richard de Tirington.
321	—	(Illegible.)	(Illegible.)
322	—	(Illegible.)	(Illegible.)
323	—	Roger Le estrange and Alice his wife by Nicolas Le estrange.	*Roger Gulafre.
324	—	William de Runhae and Agatha his wife.	Richard de Tudcham and Cecilia his wife.
325	—	*Richard de Houtone by Ralph de Reples.	Ralph and Richard sons of Wido.
326	8 John.	*Richard de Kailli.	Peter de Kailli.
327	—	*Eustace de Turgarton.	Robert le Brun.
328	—	Bartholomew de Wicton (or Witton.)	*Robert de Nugun.

Description of Property.	Consideration, &c.
.... in Houtune.	25s sterling.
The services and of half 3 acres in Walesham which she acknowledges to belong to the church of Walesham.	The regrant for ever at 7d yearly.
7 acres in	
.... in Appelton.	40s sterling.
10 acres in Cattona [Scodale (?), Leirgᵒvehill, and Billingesbi mentioned.]	The yearly rent of ....
23 acres and the half of 3 messuages in Dalling.	The regrant of 10 acres thereof, viz., a la Kirkemere, in Ethstanescroft, in Sanland, and in Crancroft, to hold for life at 20d yearly.
16 acres in Tilleneia.	Half a mark of silver.
.... in Jernemue.	4 marks of silver.
.... in Hulmo.	1 bezant.
Advowson of Sudecrec.	100s sterling.
24 acres in Ho. [Holemere mentioned.]	(?)
20 acres in Tirington of the fee of St. Etheldred.	6½ marks of silver.
18 acres in Gessing which Alice claims as reasonable dower from her late husband Simon de Franchevill.	The regrant to hold at 12d yearly, for which regrant Roger pays a mark of silver.
.... in Hokering.	
26 acres in Norbarsham—Richard calling the Prior of Acre to warrant.	The regrant of 4 acres thereof, viz., .. in Greneg .... & lying between the land of Ralph Rust (or Rutt.)
.... in Walepol.	5 marks of silver.
7 acres in Turgarton.	15d a year and Robert pays half a mark.
Advowson of Church of St. Magdalen of Warham.	18 acres in Warham.

No.	Date.	"Petens."	"Tenens."
329	8 John.	*Thomas fit Alexander.	John Achilchard.
330	—	Gena widow of Adam de Nerford.	Prior and Convent of Westacre.
331	—	*Reiner (?) de Albinico.	William Earl of Arundel.
332	—	*Richard fit Lecie by Henry de Dockinge.	William de Shireford.
333	—	Roger	*Robert de Gillingeham.
334	—	*Emma del Frid.	John del Frid.
335	—	Dameta widow of William de Rokelund.	Thomas fit Hugh de Rokelund.
336		The Prior of Norwich by Robert de Neuton.	*Robert Chaplain of Ameringhal.
337	—	(Illegible.)	
338	—	(Illegible.)	(Illegible.)
339	—	*Alex. fit Alured by John de Tunstall.	William fit Edmund.
340	—	*William de Holcham.	Peter de Bodham and Elewisa de Bodham.
341	—	Muriel widow of Wm. de Bello Monte.	*William his son.
342	—	(Illegible.)	
343		*Alice de Sparham.	John de Folesham.

Description of Property.	Consideration, &c.
8ˢ and 12ᵈ rent in Fordham and the rent of 2000 eels from the marsh of Redhebech, all of which John de Cremplesham gave to the said John in marriage with his daughter Katherine.	3 marks of silver.
Half all the land which the Prior held of Adam in Westacre.	1 mark of silver and the yearly rent of 6ᵈ.
1 knight's fee in Snetesham, Resinges, and Stanho.	£10 yearly rent. The fee to revert to Reiner if he survives William.
4 acres in Shireford.	1 mark of silver.
Advowson of Harpele.	2ᵈ rent in Nortun, which Roger Burel held.
10 acres in Tyleñ.	20ˢ sterling.
8 acres in Rokelund claimed in dower.	The regrant to Robert at 4ˢ for life, and after his death to his son John for life, and after his death to his (the latter's) wife Estrilda for life.
10 acres in Ameringhal and 8 acres in Newton.	
.... in Hokering.	
5 acres in Wichamton.	The regrant of 4 acres thereof, viz., in Uverswong, Westegate, Berchenestie, Berch, lands of Elwin Palmer, Netherlond, Buscland, Longehalfaker, and the marsh of Godinesmers at 6¼ᵈ yearly.
The yearly rent of 4 "lumar (?) bladi."	20ˢ.
Reasonable dower in Timeltorp "sic aqua descendit a novo ponte usque ad Hakefordwad."	
6 acres in Sparham which she claims in free marriage of the gift of Sculi de Sparham her father; also 6 acres in Sparham which she claims as dower of Alexander fit Decani her late husband.	16ᵈ yearly rent.

No.	Date.	"Petens."	"Tenens."
344	8 John.	*Theda wid. of Hugh Cuckuc.	Morice Forester.
345	—	Richard	*Robert fil Richard.
346	—	(Illegible.)	Roger de . . . . .
347	—	(Illegible.)	
348	—	*Godwin fil Sefugel by John de Tunstall.	William fil Edmund.
349	—	*Henry fil Leffi and Beatrice his wife.	Martin fil William.
350	—	Alexander fil Simon de Wickld.	Abbot and Convent of Dereham.
351	—	Eustace de Turgarton.	Ralph Abbot de "Ulmo."
352	—	*Richard fil Ranulph de Rissemer.	Matilda Prioress of Karhow and her convent.
353	—	*William fil Gelerani.	William Cocus.
354	—	Ralph and Peter sons of Windlevi (?)	*William Le Neuman.
355	9 John.	*William de Nuers.	Hubert de Burg by John de Ingeworth.
356	—	*Adam de Kailli.	Michael [de Ponyng.--Bl.] . . . . and Margeria his wife by Laurence de Punffinges.
357	—	*Reginald (?) de Burnham and Juliana his wife.	Hubert de Burg.

117

Description of Property.	Consideration, &c.
7 acres in Bencytleia claimed as dower.	1 mark of silver.
18 acres in Snetesham.	3 marks of silver.
20 acres in	
5 acres in Wichamtō.	The regrant of one-half, viz., in Beretrevestic, Dudegraveuverwang, Netherwonge, Westgate, Longhalfaker, and marsh of Godinesmers.
10 acres in	60^s.
Half an acre at the western side of the door of the grange of the Abbot at Holcham.	2 marks of silver.
. . . . in Turgarton—land which John Grulin held.	
A marsh called Torpigemers.	The regrant of the western half of the said Torpinggemers to hold at 12^d yearly.
A knight's fee in Kalvele.	The regrant of 24 acres, viz., in Eldeland, Stornlond (?), Langefurlong, and Wudecroft, to hold at 12^d a year. William Cocus pays 10 marks.
4 acres in Fuldon.	The regrant of one of such acres, viz., that abutting on the mill of Sudbroc, &c. (illegible.)
One-ninth of two knight's fees in Beeston and Runeton, and one-ninth of 2 carucates of land in Hindringham.	The regrant of ¼ of such 2 carucates to hold at 2^s a year, saving the dower of Sarra the widow of Ralph de Candos.
The dower of the said Margeria from her former husband John de Kailli in Bradeham, Denever, and Riston [the park of Brandenham and the old fosse mentioned] to hold to her for life.	The release of her dower in Hildeburwurth, Pikeham, Riston, and Claia.
One-ninth of two knight's fees in Beeston and Runton and one-ninth of two carucates of land in Hindringham.	100^s sterling & a robe worth 2 marks [Walter de Falcob; appon. clam. suum.]

No.	Date.	"Petens."	"Tenens."
358	9 John.	*Robert fit Raun (?) and Alice his wife by Adam de Ho.	Hubert de Burg by John de Ingeworth.
359	—	*Robert le Belage by Adam de Ho.	Hubert de Burgh by John de Ingeworth.
360	—	*Wido de Tichewelle by Nicholas de Docking.	Geoffrey fit Turstan and Matilda his wife.
361	—	Herebert Prior of Rudham by Robert de Colekerke.	*Hamo Capellanus.
362	—	*William Blund.	Wm. fit Wm. fit Roscelin.
363	—	*William Boidi son of Robert.	Richard fit Roger.
364	—	*Lecia fit Swetive.	Godefrid fit Godefrid.
365	—	*Herlewin fit Fulco.	William fit Reginald.
366	—	*Nicholas de Docking.	William fit Turstan and Goda his wife by Gaufrid fit Turstan.
367	—	*Emma de Bellafag.	Simon fit Cecil.
368	10 John.	*Reginald fit Henry.	Ralph Prior of Dunmawe.
369	—	William de Suningham and Juliana his wife.	*Hugh de Polstede and Hawisia his wife.
370	—	*Umfrid fit Turber.	Hardwin de Mortun.

Description of Property.	Consideration, &c.
One-ninth of two knights' fees in Beeston and Runeston, and one-ninth of 2 carucates of land in Hindringham.	100^s sterling [Walter de Faukberg appon. clam. suum.]
One-third of ditto.	The grant of 20 acres in Beeston and Runton, to hold by free service at 6^d yearly and the payment of 10 marks of silver.
30 acres in Docking.	5 marks of silver.
20 acres in Tivetshale, viz., juxta croftam Juliani .... Notoluesmor next the land of Ralph Coket ...... Ellernewong ...... Grepittes .... Sepegate and Fresmere.	4 marks of silver and 28^d rent.
The manor of Hciford [? Haynesford.]	The service of a knight's fee and 100^s rent payable half-yearly. Fitz Roscelin also gives a horse worth 10 marks, and returns a charter which he had of Wm. the grandfather of the said William Blund, &c.
20 acres in Tateresford.	The regrant of an acre called Gorland, abutting on the road from Dunton, to hold at a penny a year.
20 acres in Tilneia.	13^s sterling.
A messuage and 18 acres in Torp.	The regrant of the eastern half at 12^d yearly, Herlewin paying 1 mark.
30 acres in Docking.	5 marks of silver.
Various services in Flitcham. 21 acres in Hemehale which he admits to be of the right of the Prior and of the Church of St. Mary of Hemhal.	4 acres in the same town in Northfeld and Westfield.
40 acres in Saham (?)	[N.B. This is an extremely long fine, written in a foreign hand.]
2½ acres in Mortun.	Half a mark of silver.

No.	Date.	"Petens."	"Tenens."
371	10 John.	*Peter fil Hubert and Margaret his wife.	William fil Warin.
372	—	*Robert Carpentar and Alice his wife.	William de Nuers.
373	—	*Alice and Matilda the daughters of Robert de Bradefeld.	Roger fil Vitalis.
374	—	*Cristina widow of Adam de Coleby.	Reginald de Crakeford.
375	—	John le Gros.	*John fil Yvo and Margaret his mother.
376	—	*Edric de Stokesby and Wlviva his wife.	Lefflauñ de Stocinb and Matilda his wife.
377	—	Alexander de Haggeford.	*Richard de Iteringham.
378	—	*William de Iteringham.	Bartholomew de Turtevill.
379	—	*Ralph de Patesle.	Elias de Feres by Eustace his son.
380	—	*Ralph de Tivill.	Roger de Ilo.
381	—	Roger fil Nicholas	*Magister Thos. deweston.
382	—	Nicholas fil Reginald.	*Luca the Chaplain.
383	—	*Thomas fil Ralph.	Henry fil Wlnsht.
384	—	*Edmunda and Estrilda the daughters of Ailmer de Horshey by Walter Sherewind.	Josep fil Bonde.
385	—	*Cristiana widow of Geoffrey de Scotho.	Gervase de Scotho.
386	—	Steffan de Oxon.	*Closwein de Bee.
387	—	*Odo fil Eustace.	Walter fil Edmund.
388	—	*Rand fil Hugh.	Geoffrey fil Walther.

Description of Property.	Consideration, &c.
7 acres in Coleton.	Half a mark of silver.
4 acres in Hindringham.	3½ acres in Sumringate (abutting on land of Julian de Nuers) to hold at 4ᵈ yearly.
15 acres in Illegrave.	20ˢ sterling.
10 acres in Coleby.	5ˢ and an annuity of 4ᵈ.
18 acres in Geistweyt.	The regrant of 12 acres to hold at 2ˢ yearly.
9 acres in Stokingeb.	The regrant of 2 acres in the field of Stokingb to hold of the capital lord at 15ᵈ yearly.
3 acres in Matelase.	2 marks of silver.
3 acres in Wichingham.	Half a mark of silver.
A carucate of land in Rudham.	20ˢ sterling.
Half a knight's fee in Topecroft.	15 marks of silver.
7 acres in Weston to hold by free socage at 24ˢ yearly.	Thomas pays 1 mark.
10 acres in Beremere and Berewick.	The regrant to Paulin, son of Luke, and the heirs of his body at 12ᵈ yearly. Should he have no issue, to Nicholas.
2 acres in Lenn.	1 mark of silver.
3 acres in Horshey as to which Joseph calls Thomas de Thirne to warrant.	The regrant of 1 acre 3 roods thereof, viz., in Adverescroft, &c., and to hold by free service at 16ᵈ a year.
12 acres in dower from her late husband.	15ˢ sterling.
2 acres and a messuage in Geywđ (?) which he admits to belong to Stephen and the Church of St. Faith of Gaywode (?)	The regrant to Closwein for life at 12ᵈ yearly.
4 acres in Curstorp.	The regrant at 9ᵈ yearly.
40 acres in Ruieshal.	The regrant of half thereof to hold at the service of one-fortieth of a knight's fee.

No.	Date.	"Petens."	"Tenens."
389	10 John.	William Nepos.	*Ineta fit Henry.
390	—	*Wido de Sernebrune.	Nicol de Sernebrune.
391	—	*William le Perñiter and Beatrix his wife by Thomas his son.	Durand le Eschermiour.
392	—	William Prior of Norwich.	*Simon de Tornham by Gregory his brother.
393	—	*William de Anamara and Edift his wife.	Ralph de Cree.
394	—	*Richard fit Simon.	Ralph fit Emma.
395	—	*Reginald Fabr̃ de Samford.	Deodatus Prior of St. Faith by William the Monk.
396	—	*Agatha de Bovill by Peter de Lacresnere.	Cristiana de Moutencia.
397	—	*Cristiana widow of Adam de Coleby.	Simon de Crakeford.
398	—	*Robert fit Richard by Walter his son.	William fit Robert de la funteine.
399	—	*Raunulph fit William.	Roger de Ho.
400	—	*Thomas fit Ralph.	Onich fit Levesun.
401	—	*Peter fit Hubert and Margery his wife.	Hugh le Brun.
402	—	*Richard fit Ibñ by Simon his son.	William fit Richard de Mortuomar̃.
403	—	*Geoffrey de Grena.	Raunulph fit William by William his son.
404	—	*Peter de Claye.	Geoffrey Tercel.
405	—	*Ernald fit William.	Beatrix fit Agnes and Hugh her son.

Description of Property.	Consideration, &c.
8 acres in Rudham.	The regrant of 4 acres for her life at 6^d yearly.
Advowson of Sernebrune.	16^s sterling.
1½ acres in Ingham.	1 acre between the land of Bernard de Hacthorp and land of Edric Spic to hold at 6^d yearly, for which Wm. and Beatrix pay 20^s sterling.
A carucate in Tornham.	
16 acres and a messuage in Crec.	A mark of silver.
6 acres in Warham.	The regrant of 2 acres thereof in the field called sevenacre .. at 4^d yearly.
12 acres in Horsham.	3½ marks of silver.
A carucate in Trikestun claimed as dower by Cristiana from her late husband Robert le Veautre.	6 marks and 10^s.
Her dower in respect of 11 acres in Coleby.	1 mark of silver.
2 acres 1 rood and the one-third of a rood in Fileby.	The yearly rent of $4½^d$.
6 acres in Sotesham.	1 mark of silver.
3 acres in Clenchewarthon.	20^s of silver.
15 acres in Coleton.	1 mark of silver.
30 acres in Eggemer.	5 marks of silver.
2 acres of land and 2 acres of pasture in Kyrkested.	The regrant of 1 acre in Allesell next the wood of Berch at 1^d a year.
13 acres in Claye.	The regrant of 2 acres, viz., "in Cāyo q^i d^r Blackswong" to hold at 2^d a year.
4½ acres in Palling.	The regrant of half thereof, viz., in Siwatesfot ... in Lochus ...... Alfwanesherne ... Alderfanpittes ... at 6^d a year.

No.	Date.	"Petens."	"Tenens."
406	10 John.	Adam fil Reginald.	*Swetema fil Gaufr'.
407	—	Adam Cholle of Lenn.	*Richard fil John de Tilneia, and Simon, Ralph, and Godfrey his brothers.
408	—	*Richard fil Lesquen.	Safrid fil Ralph.
409	—	*Emma widow of William de Belāg.	Gervase de Parco.
410	—	William de Holebec.	*Ralph de Leonibʒ and Emma his wife.
411	—	*Walter fil Robert Brito.	Thomas La Veile.
412	—	Walter Le Brun.	*Ralph de Fueldon.
413	—	*William fil Hugh.	Wido de Verdun and Wm de Holkham.
414	—	*Alveva widow of Gilbert.	Richard Earl of Clare by Hugh de Bodekesham his "athornatus."
415	—	*William fil Walter.	Reginald de Sumere.
416	—	*Marcelina widow of Richard Cameraṙ by Robert fil Macelin.	Richard le Awe by Richard his son.
417	—	Humfrey fil Turbeṙ.	*Ralph fil Leffy.
418	—	*Aliva widow of Gilbert.	Richard Earl of Clare by Hugh de Clar.
419	—	Roger fil Osbert.	*William de Curzun.
420	—	*Stephen de Warham.	Geoffrey fil Peter de Warham.
421	—	*Walter Faber de Saxford.	Deodatus Prior of St. Faith.

Description of Property.	Consideration, &c.
4 acres in Toft.	The regrant of 2 acres, viz., in Westmad ... Michelbrom ... to hold at 3ˢ yearly.
20 acres in Tilneia and Wigehal.	Half a mark of silver.
10 acres in Stratton.	The regrant of 2 acres in Piggestoft abutting on Stanahage.
16 acres in Baldeswell.	20ˢ sterling.
7 acres in Wikingeham.	The regrant of half thereof at 18ᵈ yearly.
40 acres in Bastwic.	1 mark argent.
Half a carucate in Fueldon.	The regrant of all except 3 acres, viz., in Erdehou ... Schirevesacr̃ ... Galecho.
12 acres in Saxlingham.	Regrant of 3½ acres ... to hold at 4ᵈ yearly and scutage.
1½ acres in Bodekesham.	Half the croft called Ailevescroft ... Micloweye to hold at 2ˢ yearly.
7 acres in Sumere.	2 marks of silver.
20 acres in Hadesco (?)	2½ acres in ... Ranescroft abutting on Wadegrote to hold at ½ᵈ yearly.
1 acre in Morton.	Half the said acre to hold at 1½ᵈ yearly.
1½ acres in Rodokesham.	Half the croft called Alevescroft.
2 carucates in Wicklingham of the fee of Earl Roger le Bigot (saving to Roger Cocus his tenement, viz., 40 acres for which he is to pay 8ˢ sterling, and also saving to Mamo (?) de Kirkley his tenement of 12 acres, for which he is to pay 2ˢ and two capons.)	The service of two knights' fees and £14 and ½ a mark.
15 acres in Warham.	Regrant of 2 acres in the field called Foxhalls at 6ᵈ yearly.
12 acres in Horsham.	3 marks of silver.

No.	Date.	"Petens."	"Tenens."
422	10 John.	Godfrey del acre.	*William de Scales.
423	—	Richard Parmentar.	*Reginald de Crakeford.
424	—	*John Coleman and Roger his brother by Henry fit William.	William de Eggesfeld.
425	—	*Peter fit Hubert and Margaret his wife.	Hageñ fit Warin.
426	—	*Richard de Bedsted.	Hil[ary] Prior of [Lew]es by Richard Coleman.
427	—	*William fit Benedict.	Roger fit Reginald.
428	—	Richard fit Ibert by Simon his son.	Adam fit Elie.
		Ditto.	Ralph fit Bartholomew.
		Ditto.	John Mercator.
		Ditto.	Amabilia fit Elie.
429	—	*Aleysia fit William.	William Brun and Alan fit William.
430	—	*Gervase de Sparham and Amicia his wife and Agnes her sister.	Geoffrey Palmere.
431	—	*Ralph fit Henry.	William fit Geoffrey and Muriel his wife.
432	—	*Gervase de Scotho.	John fit Geoffrey.
433	—	Gilbert Abbot of Langley.	*Roger Bacun, and Walter de Raveningham, and Reiner (?) de Ho, and Ernald de Charnell, and William de Ingelose, and Reginald de Brokel, and Ralph de Bello Campo.

Description of Property.	Consideration, &c.
30 acres in Rucham.	The regrant of half at 11^d yearly, excepting the capital messuage which is to remain to William, in exchange for which he gives Godfrey an acre on Galterhill next the land of Thomas fit Scul.
1 acre in Skegeton.	20^s sterling.
2 acres in Adelmerton.	The regrant of 1 acre, viz., which lies next the road called Pakkeresfaillate, to hold at 3^d yearly.
7 acres in Coleton.	Half a mark of silver.
6 acres in Waletou.	3½ marks of silver.
Half of a mill and ½ of an acre in Refham.	The regrant at 2^d yearly, Roger paying 10^s.
. . . in Eggemere. 10 acres in ditto. 7 perches in ditto. 1 acre in ditto.	A long and complicated fine.
30 acres in . . . [torn.]	The regrant of a rod of land abutting on Taseburgland . . . and on Lampit . . . on land of Hervey le Spicer, and half an acre at Uveregate, and 30^s.
3 acres in Sparham.	3^s sterling.
30 acres in Sailtwert.	1 mark of silver.
3 acres in Scotho. Advowson of three parts of the Church of the Holy Trinity of Lodnes.	Nil.

No.	Date.	"Petens."	"Tenens."
434	10 John.	*Robert fil Ralph and Matilda his wife.	Henry fil Robert and Basilia his wife.
435	—	*Peter fil Hubert.	Henry Abbot of Dereham.
436	—	*Robert le Gris.	William de Watacre.
437	—	*Richer fil Geoffrey.	Gilbert fil Geoffrey.
438	—	*Edina fil Ulph.	Raunulf Capell.
439	—	*Wimarca fil Osbert.	William fil Richard.
440	—	Geoffrey de Naringes.	*Alan de Heleghton by William his son.
441	—	*Roger fil Haldan.	Godfrey fil Roger.
442	—	*Ralph de Clay and Agnes his wife.	Walter de Witton.
443	—	*Richard fil Ralph.	Philip de Bodeham.
444	—	Ralph fil Warin.	*Hugh Swan.
445	—	*William fil Robert.	Jordan fil William.
446	—	*William le Neuman.	Philip Prior of Acre.
447	—	*John fil Robert.	Robert de Haldsted.
448	—	*Seman Capellanus.	Hugh Plume.
449	—	John fil Alice.	*William de Kelechou and Edina his wife.
450	—	Albina Yreneto & Beatrice and Ediva her sisters by William de Brom.	*Simon de Erwelleston.

Description of Property.	Consideration, &c.
5 acres in Snetesham.	1 mark of silver.
20 acres in Ysted and 13ᵈ rent in Weibrede.	2 marks of silver.
15ˢ rent in Torton.	
14 acres in Wichingeham.	1 mark of silver.
4 acres in Aracton.	Half a mark of silver.
1 carucate in Lornedis (? Launditch.)	2 marks of silver and the grant to her son Ranulph of 3 acres of the said land, viz., that which Goding May held at 18ᵈ yearly.
1 carucate in Helgheton.	The regrant at 18ˢ a year, Alan pays 12 marks.
7 acres in Grimueston.	The regrant of 4 acres, to hold at 12ᵈ.
2 carucates in Witton and Warham.	The grant of 36 acres and 3 poles in Warham which Yward Presbiter held of Bartholomew, father of the said Walter de Witton, to hold to him and the heirs of Agnes at 12ᵈ yearly.
6 acres in Cree.	The regrant to hold at 12ᵈ yearly.
9 acres in Bicham.	1 mark of silver.
3 acres in Stratton.	Ditto.
22 acres in Baggethorp.	3 marks of silver.
40 acres in Heveye.	10 marks of silver.
7 acres in Aslacton.	The regrant of 5½ acres, viz., at Bradeland .... Litlewell .. Michelemadfurlong ... a wood called Frunteshage ... a toft called Frunteseroft .... and in la Breche to hold at 11ᵈ yearly.
3 acres in Dimmenethoũ.	20ᵈ sterling.
15 acres in Kyrkeby.	38ˢ.

No.	Date.	"Petens."	"Tenens."
451	10 John.	Thomas de Keneteford and Margaret his wife.	*Hugh de Bodekesham.
452	—	*Robert fil Osbert.	Simon fil Robert.
453	—	*John Symīg.	Thomas Duin.
454	—	*John fil Richard.	Alexander, Nicholas, and Roger, sons of Robert.
455	—	Simon de Algeto.	*William de Bee.
456	—	*Roisia de Ruieshal.	Stephen Blund and Agnes his mother.
457	—	*Robert de Say.	Gilbert de Stowe.
458	—	*William de Fraxineto.	Walter de Hatfeld.
459	—	*Elias fil Ralph.	Hardewin de Mortun and William his son.
460	—	*Robert de Glanvill.	William de Egefeld.
461	—	*William fil Osbert.	Robert Capellanus.
462	—	*William fil Osbert.	Roger Lefled.
463	—	*Richard fil Roger.	Roger fil Robert.
464	—	*Robert Foke (? Toke)	Roger de Bosco.
465	—	*Margeria de Ludham.	Ralph le Bret.
466	—	*Bernard Bauman.	Simon de Ormesby and Letitia his mother, widow of Roger.
467	—	*Tomas fil Ralph.	Astyn fil Currichīt.

Description of Property.	Consideration, &c.
Half a virgate of land and 6 acres in Bodekesham.	The regrant at 10ˢ a year.
2 messuages in Welles.	The regrant of ½ (except 5 acres and 1 rood at Waxsebeche) at 4ᵈ yearly.
12 acres in Barsham.	The regrant of ½ (except the capital messuage) at 12ᵈ yearly; in exchange for which messuage Thos. gives 1 acre 1 rood at Prestmere.
12 acres in Thritton.	20ˢ sterling.
1 carucate in Folesham.	The regrant of 10ˢ 8ᵈ, for which regrant William pays 20 marks of silver.
Half a carucate in Saxlingham.	A mark of silver.
20 acres in Stowe.	2 marks of silver [William fit Gerbode puts in the claim of Vacilla his wife.]
A carucate in Ess.	50ˢ sterling [Osbert de Wachesham puts in his claim.]
2 acres in ..... as to which the tenants call Deodatus, Prior of St. Faith, to warrant.	10ˢ. Hardwin and Wm. to hold of the Prior at 2ᵈ yearly.
A carucate in Ructon. Wm. calls Earl Roger Bigot to warrant. Robert quits claim to the Earl, who pays 40 marks of silver, and the land is to remain to the tenant and his heirs, who are to hold of the Earl at the service of a knight's fee.	
14 acres in Brokedis.	24ˢ sterling.
20 acres in Tructon [? Thuxton]	1 mark.
12 acres in Saxlingham and Dalling.	20ˢ sterling.
7 acres in Reppes.	The regrant of the eastern half.
20 acres in Morle to hold for life, with remainder to the grantor.	
2 acres in Ormesby.	The regrant of an acre thereof in Westtoft and Westgate to hold at ½ᵈ yearly.
4 acres in Clenchwarton.	2 marks of silver.

No.	Date.	"Petens."	"Tenens."
468	11 John.	*Lecenta fil Elflet by Laurence de Stocton.	Roger Anketel.
469	—	*Alice widow of Robert Cholle by Eudo Norensis.	Jocelina de Walpol by Robert de Tyrinton.
470	—	*Philip le Morice.	Berenger Moure.
471	—	Adam de Carduis by Stephen fil William.	*John Blund.
472	—	Hugh de St. Philibert.	*Ralph de Longwad.
473	—	Emma de Hulmo by Wm. fil Geoffrey.	*Robert fil Richard.
474	—	Hugh de St. Philibert.	*William de Ware.
475	—	*Ralph de Cameis.	Ralph de Roneccestr̃.
476	—	*Alan de Engelfeld.	Muriel de Langetot by Jordan de Turnay.
477	—	*Thomas de Benefeld by Richard fil John.	Walter de Bergh.

Description of Property.	Consideration, &c.
7 acres in Thorp.	The regrant of half thereof, viz., 1 acre 1 rood in cultur̄ de Gosegras ... in cultura de Redhandel... near the Church of Thorp, to hold at 12^d yearly.
12 acres in Walpole.	The grant of 6 acres in Tilneia in the field called Sibilie, between the land of Adam Cholle and the land of John fil Jocelin, at 9^d yearly.
3½ hides in Thiring. † Philip pays 40 marks of silver.	The grant of all the land in Grasham which Berenger holds of the fee of Nigel de Luvetot, except the homage and service of Henry de Chodham. Also 30 acres in the same town held of the honor of Gloucester, viz., in Pratescroft, &c.†
8 acres in Boyton, Sotesham, and Saxlingham.	4 marks of silver.
Half a mill in Caldecote.	The regrant at 3^s a year, for which Ralph pays half a mark.
Half a carucate in Titleshal claimed by Emma as dower from her late husband Richard fil Robert .... in Muckole between the land of Philip de Verly and the land of Edric mercator ..... at Ingemer̄ ..... the pasture of Burland ..... the wood called Ridchage ..... at Flaxmere .... at Wunstanesnab .... at Westris, to hold to Emma for life.	
A mill in Caldecote.	The regrant of half at 3^s a year, for which William pays half a mark.
A knight's fee in Berton and Estmora.	85 marks of silver.
A carucate in Binnetre.	The grant of the whole town of Hachetot with the advowson of the Church, to hold to the "said" Alan fil Muriell at 15^s yearly.
The advowson of the Church of St. Andrew of Bergh juxta Heingham.	3 marks of silver.

No.	Date.	" Petens."	" Tenens."
478	11 John.	Adam de Mundeford.	*Roger fit Baudewin de Frivill.
479	—	*Robert fit Hugh.	Hubert de Burg by John de Ingeworth.
480	—	*Richard de la lund and Vincent, Hugh, and Thomas his brothers.	Gilbert fit Nicholas.
481	—	*Emma de Belagh by Roger her son.	Hugh de Milleres.
482	12 John.	*John fit Geoffrey.	William Prior of Buttele.
483	—	*Thomas Faber by Hugh his son.	Peter Sutor.
484	—	John fit Bernard and Sibilia his wife by Hugh fit Robert.	*John de Rocheford.
485	—	Alan de Stokesby.	*William de Redham.
486	—	*John de Reinestorp.	Robert de Tasburg.
487	—	*Nichs. fit Reginald.	Herbert Prior of Cockesford.

Description of Property.	Consideration, &c.
20ˢ rent in Letton and Sipedham.	The regrant to hold at half a mark of silver.
One-third of a knight's fee in Beston and Runeton, and one-third of 2 carucates in Hindringham.	The regrant of the said one-third at 6ˢ yearly, saving to Sarra widow of Ralph de Caudoz her dower. She comes before the justices and disclaims it.
Half a carucate in Sutrepples, viz., all which Richard Diachonus held there.	The regrant of half thereof and the payment to Gilbert of 20ˢ sterling.
10ˢ rent and 2 acres of land in Dallinges and Geistweic.	9ˢ sterling.
Half the advowson of Gissinges.	The reception of John & his heirs into all the benefits of the said monastery.
A messuage and ½ an acre in Holt. Peter calls Robert de Binetre and Matilda his wife to warrant. Ralph, Matilda's brother, comes to warrant; Thomas also quits claim of 17 acres in Holt, which Copmannus his uncle formerly held, and receives 4 marks of silver.	
Advowson of St. Gregory in Manacroft (Norwich.)	
30 acres in Stokesby.	Half a mark of silver and †
One-fifth of a knight's fee in Taseburg.	
† The grant of 10 acres in Godwinescroft and the services of Roger fit William de Molendino de Mersmelne, of William fil Robert, and 1 acre which Robert Fucher held with him and all his following, and ½ acre which Lefricus faber held with him and all his following, and 4½ acres which Richard Carpentar held with him and all his following, and ½ an acre which Ralph Textor held in villenage, and 1 acre which Richard Ording held in villenage, and ½ an acre which William Derling held in villenage.	
Half a carucate in Rudham and Beremer.	100ˢ sterling.

No.	Date.	"Petens."	"Tenens."
488	12 John.	*Philip de Bñh (torn away) by (torn) de Dunton.	William (torn), de Gyney?
489	13 John.	William de Witewell and Claricia his wife.	William de Skegeton.
490	—	Herlewin fit Fulco by Thomas de Ho.	*William fit Reginald.
491	—	Earl Roger le Bigot by Hamo Le enveise.	*Jordan le Claver.
492	—	Herbert Prior of Cokesford by Robert Joie.	*Robert de Cree and Agnes his wife by John de Glanvill.
493	—	Agnes, widow of John fit Sigar.	Mathew fit John.
494	—	Ralph Abbot of Saveny by Robert de Stratford the monk.	*Peter fit John de Dallinges.
495	—	*Erneburga widow of Hubert de Eia by William her son.	Mazelina de Norwic and Walter Knotte.
496	—	*Roger de Butemñt and Petronilla his wife.	Roger de Lenham.
497	—	*William Bigot and Margaret his wife by Reiner de Gloz.	Hugh de Herleberge.
498	—	*Hugh de Skerdeston.	Fulco Bainard by William Bainard.
499	14 John.	Raunulph de Schelton.	*Wido de ....

Description of Property.	Consideration, &c.
A mill in Witewell, which Matilda de Gyney, the mother of the said William, held in dower.	The grant to Frarinus, the brother of the said Philip, to erect a water mill in Hackeford, &c., water rights, &c.
Half of two parts of two knights' fees in Skegeton, Crostweit, and Beiton, which Claricia claims as heir to her uncle Richard.	[This is a long mutilated fine. Hugh de Schegeton the father of Claricia is mentioned; also the advowson of Skegeton.]
3¼ acres in Torp which Herlwin claims to be part of 9 acres which William granted him by fine in the 9th year of the present king, viz., at Hedenesho and in Scwardescroe.	The half acre in Hedenesho to remain to William and his heirs.
15 acres in Freton and Herdewic.	The regrant at 10^s yearly.
The fish (?) pool and vineyard of the said Prior of Torp. Interests which the Canons had of Roger de Glanville mentioned.	7^s yearly. Water rights mentioned.
Half of 40 acres in Craneworth.	The regrant of 6 acres, viz., at Dunehersewang .... Kingescroft .. Beterhuscroft ... Langethcihage ... &c.
100 acres in Dallinges which William, formerly Abbot of Saveny, granted to the said Peter and John his father by a fine dated the 6th year.	18 marks of silver.
3 acres 1 rood in Lakenham.	2 marks of silver.
2½ knights' fees in Therning and Redenhal.	15 marks of silver. Odo de Angerny and Robert de Mathon are named.
Half a knight's fee in Prilleston.	5 marks.
A debt of 30 marks.	3 marks.
16 acres in Meringethorpe and Herdewic.	The regrant of 9 acres in Bernes .... to hold at 5^d yearly.

No.	Date.	"Petens."	"Tenens."
500	14 John.	Alice widow of Herbert de Hillingeton.	*Roger fil Herebert.
501	—	Ralph Abbot of Savenñ.	*Leviva fit Ulf.
502	—	*Rogere le Fevere and Beatrix his wife by Reiner de Gloz.	Isabel de Stodeia (who calls Burnard Parson of Stodeia to warrant.)
503	—	Idem. *Lambert Thentbonitu.	Idem. Bertram de Verdun (who calls Earl Roger Bigod to warrant, who puts William de Herdeberge in his place.)
504	15 John.	*Mabil widow of Ludowic de Gurnay by Waren de Rising.	Thomas fit Ludowic.
505	—	Simon de Wahull.	*William de Hamsted.
506	—	(Illegible.)	(Illegible.)
507	16 John.	*Alan de Wigehal.	Simon de Stowe.
	—	Ditto.	Kenestan de West Winech by Hugh de Buketon.
508	—	*Beatrix widow of	Godfrey ....
509	—	Richard Prior of Binham.	*John fit Bernard & Sibilla his wife.

Description of Property.	Consideration, &c.
Half of 7 acres and half of a messuage in Heeham, and half 30 acres in Hillingeton claimed as dower ..... Hillington water mill.	The rent of 3^s 7^d yearly.
7 acres in Dallinges and all her claim to half the windmill which Roger Bacun held in the same town.	The regrant for her life of 6 acres, viz., a croft at Northgate and a "placia" called Blacunldehcved-land, and a "placia" called Stanhou, to hold at 12^d yearly and two capons at Christmas, and a "placia" called Suñndesacr.
30 acres in Bacton held of the Prior and Convent of Norwich, to hold to her and her son Geoffrey and the latter's heirs, with remainder to her daughter Beatrix.	
A mill in Hunworth called Skerchunger.	
100^s rent in Melton, which are quit claimed to the Earl.	100 marks of silver.
Half . . . acres in Cranewurth, and half 12 acres of meadow and pasture, and half a mill and a quarter of a water mill, and half 5 marks of rent in Letton, claimed as dower.	An allotment of certain land in satisfaction and 28^s 8^d. Richard de Rising, Roger le Swatinges, and John fil Brixi are named.
The service of a knight's fee which he held of Simon in Hainsted and Holt, and 3½ marks of silver, and all his claim in the service of 4^s 4^d and a pair of gloves which he received of tenants of Isolda fil Parmel, in Kent.	The release of all arrears of service.
.... Tilneia .... Islingeton.	
9 acres in Seche.	5 marks [Reginald fil Simon puts in his claim.]
3 acres in ditto.	2 marks.
One-third of 2 acres in Tilneia.	5^s sterling.
Advowson of Berneia.	The admission of the grantors into all the benefits of the monastery.

No.	Date.	"Petens."	"Tenens."
510	16 John.	John fit Hugh by Roger de Stratton.	*Roger de Clare and Wulviva his wife by William de Hemmesby.
511*	11 John.	*Richard fam̃ Roger de Wlfreton and Matilda his wife.	Matthew Clerk de Danby.
512*	—	*Aliva widow of Reiner Perm̃tar.	Simon fil Robt. and Roger fil Godland de Well.

* These two fines were by mistake of the calendarer placed and numbered after No. 510, through his mis-reading "undecimo" "vicesimo," and forgetting the duration of John's reign. On my pointing this out, they have been placed with the other fines of 11 John.

Description of Property.	Consideration, &c.
7 acres in Ormesby and an admission that they have no right to the Church of St. Margaret of Ormesby.	The regrant of 5 acres to hold to them and the heirs of Wulviva at 6ˢ yearly, and of 2 acres, viz., 1 in Brakeholm and another between the land of the Church and the land of Richard fit Wulford, to remain to John.
4 acres and a salt pit in Babbingel.	Half a mark of silver.
4 acres in suburb of Lenn, claimed as dower.	The regrant for her life of 2 acres thereof.

INDEX LOCORUM.

N.B.—For remarks as to the probable locality of the unidentified places printed in italics see page ix.

Acre Priory, 113
Alburgh, or Aldborough (?), 71
Alderford, 51
Alingeton, 15
Alpington, 113
Aracton, 129
Arminghall, 115
Ashby cum Oby, 19
Ashby, 53
Ashill, 107 (?), 131 (?)
Aslacton, 129
Attleborough, 23, 41, 49
Attlebridge, 51
Aylmerton, 37, 81, 127

Babingley, 141
Bacton, 139
Bagthorpe, 25, 129
Banham, 109
Banningham, 23, 105
Barford, 93
Barmer, 75, 97, 121, 135
Barney, 29, 139
Barnham, 23
Barningham, 71, 105, 109
Barsham, 59, 131
Barsham, North, 113
Barton, 95
Barwick, 75, 97, 121
Bastwick, 125, also see Woodbastwick
Bawdeswell, 125
Beckham, 105
Beechamwell, 71
Beeston, 83
Beeston St. Lawrence, 137 (?)
Beeston Regis, 117 bis, 118, 135
Beetley, 111
Beighton, 93
Bencytleia, 117
Bergh Apton, 75 (?)
Berton, 83, 133
Besthorpe, 23
Bexwell, 109
Bicham, 129

Billingesbi, 113
Billockby, 59, 81
Bilney, 99
Binham, 17
Bintry, 61, 133
Bittering, 81, 93
Blakeworde, 11
Blofield, 23, 39
Bodokesham, 125 bis, 131
Bodham, 71, 105, 109
Booton, 133, 137 (?)
Bradenham, 83, 117
Bramerton, 105
Brandeston, 55
Brandon, 35, 53, 103
Bressingham, 57, 95
Brettenham, 31, 53, 99
Brisley, 13
Brockdish, 131
Broome, 97
Brunsthorpe, 45
Buckenham, 31, 95
Buckenham, Old, 87
Bunwell, 41, 71
Burgh, 13, 111
Burgh juxta Heingham, 133
Burgh by Aylsham, 81
Burlingham, 23, 25, 99, 103
Burnham, 23, 33, 39, 73, 93 bis, 95, 99, 105
Burnham Thorpe, 47, 65
Burston, 11, 85, 99

Caistor, 31
Caldecote, 77, 133 bis
Caldwell, 17
Calvele, see Kelvele
Cantley, 33
Carbrooke, 85
Carleton Rode, 71, 101
Carlton, 9, 75, 85, 89, 95, 107, 111
Catton, 59, 83, 111, 113
Cawston, 35 bis
Chedestane, 91
Cherwelleston, 87

Clenchwarton, 17, 123, 131
Cley, 31, 79, 117, 123
Clipesthorp, 103
Clippesby, 13, 25, 49, 77, 81
Colby, 65, 69, 89, 95, 119, 123
Colney, 19
Colton, 55, 85, 93, 121, 123, 127
Colveston, 83
Congham, 63
Corpusty, 15, 21, 81
Cotes, 83
Cranworth, 137, 139
Creake, 9, 13, 19, 35, 37, 41, 55, 107, 123, 129
Creake, South, 37, 113
Crimplesham, 71
Crostwight, 137
Croxton, 99
Custhorpe, 121

Dalling, 9, 53, 59, 89, 91, 107, 111, 113, 131, 135, 137, 139
Denver, 69, 117
Deopham, 37
Dereham, East, 31, 73, 83
Diewude, 75
Dinunethon, 129
Docking, 11, 119 bis
Drayton, 17
Dudwic, 55
Dunham, 53, 71
Dunstale, 55
Dunston, 55, 57, 91
Dunton, 11, 25

Earlham, 15
Easton, 95
Egleston, 9
Egmere, 123, 127
Ellingham, 13, 19, 23, 49, 73, 85, 109
Elmham, 61
Erpingham, 67

Erwclestun, 95
Ess, 131
Estmora, 133

Felmingham, 69
Felthorpe, 51
Feltwell, 9, 31
Filby, 93, 107, 123
Fincham, 73 (?)
Finehele, 71
Flitcham, 47, 119
Flockthorpe, 59
Fordham, 71, 115
Forncett, 65
Fotestone, 107
Foulden, 117, 125
Foulsham, 131
Fransham, 45, 79
Frenze, 13
Frettenham, 93
Fring, 27, 31, 39, 73 bis, 87
Fritton, 35, 77, 79, 137
Fulmodeston, 107 (?)
Fundenhall, 83

Gateley, 27, 73, 87, 103
Gayton, 59
Gaywood, 121
Gillingham, 39
Gissing, 13, 113, 135
Glosebrīg, 9
Grenesvill, 11
Gresham, 133
Grimstone, 17, 19, 21, 23, 41, 43, 83, 111, 129
Grovele, 85
Guestwick, 73, 121, 135
Gunton, 109

Hachetot, 133
Hackford, 29, 69, 115, 137
Hadestune, 43, 55, 59, 65
Haddiscoe, 125
Hainford, 25, 79, 119 (?)
Hales, 57
Hardley, 89
Hardwick, 31, 43, 137 bis
Hargham, 77
Haringeshang, 97
Harpley, 103, 115
Heacham, 9, 71, 73, 103, 139
Heckford, 119
Hechamthorp, 109
Heckingham, 33, 51
Helhoughton, 77, 129

Hellesdon, 15, 27
Helmingham, 15
Hempnall, 111, 119
Hempstead, 71, 139 (?)
Herringby, 15
Heveye, 129
Heveringland, 33
Heydon, 11
Hickling, 109
Hikeford, 35
Hilborough, 117
Hildeburchworth, 67
Hilgay, 71
Hillington, 15 (?), 29, 35, 139
Hindolveston, 51
Hindringham, 117 bis, 119, 121, 135
Hingham, 11, 47
Hockering, 111, 113, 115
Hockwold, 31
Hoe, 113
Holkham, 117
Holme, 19, 83, 113
Holt, 81, 135, 139
Honingham, 75
Horningtoft, 29, 109
Horsey, 75, 121
Horsham, 123, 125
Horstead, 27, 37, 55, 97
Horstun, 97
Houghton, 43, 65, 87, 95, 113
Hueton, 85
Hulm, 15
Humesfield, 61
Hunstanton, 13
Hunworth, 139

Ickburgh, 61, 71
Illegrave, 121 (? Hilgay)
Illington, 21
Ingham, 123
Inland, 87
Irstead, 129 (?)
Islington, 17, 55, 73, 87, 139
Itteringham, 81

Kalvete, 117
Karboisthorpe, 37
Kikelington, 29
Kilverstone, 99
Kimberley, 49, 79
Kinesthorp, 59
Kirby, 19, 95, 129
Kirstead, 123
Knardeston, 83
Kyneholm, 55

Lakenham, 137

Langham, 41
Launditch, 71, 129
Letton, 35, 135, 139
Lexham, 19
Limpenhoe, 15, 43, 101
Lingwood, 29
Litcham, 19
Littleholm, 17
Loddon, 23, 97, 127
Lopham, 29, 53, 83
Lowringeham, 59
Lynford, 71
Lynn, E., 107 (?)
Lynn, North, 39 bis
Lynn, 17, 21 bis, 25 bis, 27, 35 bis, 37, 39 bis, 51 bis, 53 (4), 57, 61, 63, 65 (3), 69, 73, 83, 85, 91, 97, 105, 109 (3), 111, 121, 141

Marham, 71
Marlingford, 49, 107
Martham, 23, 47
Massingham, 83, 93
Matlask, 21, 121
Mautby, 27, 37
Melton, 45, 67, 139
Mendham, 33
Metton, 15
Middleton, 25
Morley, 71, 105, 131
Morton, 51, 119, 125
Moulton, 17, 35, 97
Morningthorpe, 27, 101, 137
Mulbarton, 81 (? see Berton)
Mundford, 89
Mundham, 21

Narford, 95
Nesse, 9
Newcater, 11
Newton, 67, 115
Norcot, 85
Northton, 9
Norton, 15, 83, 97, 115
Norwich, Suburbs of, 111
Norwich, St. Peter Mancroft, 135

Ormesby, 49, 75, 131, 141
Osmondeston, 19
Oulton, 25, 47
Outwell, 73
Ovington, 85
Oxburgh, 103

Puggrave, 75
Pulling, 123
Punkesford, 99
Pickenham, 51, 117
Piruho, 19
Plumstead, 39, 71, 105
Prilleston, 107, 137

Quiddenham, 58, 69, 97

Rackheath, 17, 101
Rainham, 61, 73, 97
Rainham, S, 61
Rainthorpe, 67
Raveningham, 85, 111
Redenhall, 67, 137
Reedham, 101
Reepham, 111, 127
Repps, 19, 131
Repps, South, 135
Reston, 73
Richam, 129
Riding (Rising?), 57
Ringstead, 13, 57, 95
Rising, 57 (?), 115
Rockland, 25, 35, 115
Rocton, 11
Roudham, 51
Rougham, 27, 77, 127
Roxham, 71
Rudham, 23, 35, 55, 121, 123, 135
Runhall, 45, 51
Runham, 53
Runton, 117 bis, 119, 131, 135
Rushall, 13, 41, 77, 91, 107, 121
Rutlinghall, 15
Ryburgh, 45, 69
Ryburgh Parva, 65, 101, 107
Ryston, 117 bis

Saddlebow, 23
Saham, 119
Sailwert (?), 127
Sall, 21
Santon, 107
Saxlingham, 4 bis, 61, 82, 27, 125, 131 bis, 133
Scottow, 127
Setchy, 45, 71, 87, 105, 139
Sharrington, 17
Shelfhanger, 57
Shelton, 73
Shereford, 11 bis, 115
Shernborne, 123
Shipden, 15, 35, 83

Shipdham, 135
Shotisham, 85, 105, 123, 133
Shouldham, 73
Shropham, 37
Skeyton, 127, 137
Snitterton, 13
Snettisham, 15, 19, 43, 87, 115, 117, 129
Socestone (?), 107
Somerton, 37, 79, 109
Southery, 73
Southmere, 125
Sparham, 9, 55, 115, 127
Spixworth, 65
Stanford, 11
Stanhoe, 75, 97, 115
Stibbard, 101
Stikingeland, 105
Stokesby (Stokingby?), 121, 135
Stow, 27, 59, 131
Stradsett, 71
Stratton, 11, 23, 41, 69, 73, 77, 83, 89, 93, 95, 125, 129
Sudmere, 55, 69
Suffield, 19, 83
Surlingham, 49, 73
Swaffham, 59
Swainsthorpe, 9, 29, 79, 105
Swanington, 51 bis, 73
Swanton, 17, 25, 49, 67
Swardeston, 75
Syderstone, 41, 51, 67

Tacolnestone, 15, 21, 65, 111
Tasburgh, 61, 103, 135
Tatterford, 119
Taverham, 51
Tering, or *Toring*, 9
Terrington, 9, 31, 71, 113
Thelton, 23
Themelthorpe, 115
Thornham, 21, 59, 123
Thorpe, 71, 75, 95, 101, 119, 133, 137
Threxton, 123
Thurgarton, 113, 117
Thurmodeston, 89
Thurne, 41
Thurning, 11, 133, 137
Thurton, 39, 131 (?)
Thuxton, 131 (?)
Tibbenham, 59, 71, 101
Tilbury, 91

Tilney, 15, 17, 19, 23, 41, 57, 71, 75, 95, 111, 113, 115, 119, 125, 133
Tilney - cum - Islington, 139 bis
Titchwell, 21
Tittleshall, 43, 103, 133
Tivetshall, 13, 33, 79, 81, 107, 119
Toft, 41, 49, 99, 107, 125
Topcroft, 121
Torpingemers, 117
Tottington, 13 bis, 23, 29
Tuddenham, East, 17, 45
Tuddenham, West, 17
Tunethorp, 111
Tunstall, 11, 39
Tunstead, 37, 57
Twai, 111

Upton, 13

Wacton, 49
Walpole, 113, 133
Walsham, 15, 27 bis
Walsham, North, 9, 27, 105, 113
Walsingham Magna, 69, 107, 111
Walsoken, 35, 71, 87, 93
Walton, 17, 33 (?), 43, 47, 127
Warham, 113, 123, 125, 129
Waxham, 95, 105, 109
Weasenham, 53 bis
Weybread, 129
Welle, 63, 109, 111
Wellingham, 59
Wells, 27, 47, 69 bis, 97, 103, 109, 131
Westacre, 71, 115
Weston, 55, 121
Whissonsett, 9, 29
Whitwell, 137
Wiclesford, 107
Wicherestorp, 83
Wickhampton, 115, 117
Wicklewood, 51, 81 bis
Wiggenhall, 17, 19, 31 bis, 33, 41, 53, 55 (?), 71, 79, 125
Wighton, 59, 61, 67, 75
Wimbotsham, 83, 89, 109, 111
Winch, West, 31, 45, 55, 65, 73, 79, 83, 91, 105, 109, 111
Winterton, 37, 59, 109

L

Witchingham, 11, 25, 27, 35, 51, 61, 85, 107 bis, 121, 125, 129
Whitlingham, 125 (?)
Witton, 29, 31, 97, 129
Wolterton, 9, 13, 27 ?), 71
Woodbastwick, 107, 125
Wood Dalling, 121
Woodrow, 4
Woodton, 75, 99
Wootton, 33 ?)
Wramplingham, 101
Wretham, 63
Wretton, 11
Wymondham, 101
Yarmouth, 23, 61, 67, 113
Yaxham, 65
Yelverton, 27
Ykeburg, 71

www.ingramcontent.com/pod-product-compliance
Lightning Source LLC
Chambersburg PA
CBHW020310170426
43202CB00008B/564